JAMES CAGNEY

The Pictorial Treasury of Film Stars

JAMES CAGNEY

by

Andrew Bergman

General Editor: **TED SENNETT**

GALAHAD BOOKS • NEW YORK CITY

This Galahad Books edition is published by
arrangement with Pyramid Communications, Inc.

Copyright © 1973 by Pyramid Communications, Inc.

ISBN 0-88365-162-9

Library of Congress Catalog Card Number 73-90215

Printed in the United States of America

PREFACE

By Ted Sennett

"The movies!" Flickering lights in the darkness that stirred our imaginations and haunted our dreams. All of us cherish memories of "going to the movies" to gasp at feats of derring-do, to roar with laughter at clownish antics, to weep at acts of noble sacrifice. For many filmgoers, the events on the screen were not only larger than life but also more mysterious, more fascinating, and—when times were bad—more rewarding. And if audiences could be blamed for preferring movies to life, they never seemed to notice, or care.

Of course the movies have always been more than a source of wish-fulfillment or a repository for nostalgic memories. From the first unsteady images to today's most experimental efforts, motion pictures have mirrored America's social history, and over the decades they have developed into an internationally esteemed art.

As social history, movies reflect our changing tastes, styles, and ideas. To our amusement, they show us how we looked and behaved: flappers with bobbed hair and bee-stung lips cavorting at "wild" parties; gangsters and G-men in striped suits and wide-brimmed hats exchanging gunfire in city streets; pompadoured "swing-shift" Susies and dashing servicemen, "working for Uncle Sam." To our chagrin, they show us the innocent (and sometimes not so innocent) lies we believed: that love triumphs over all adversity and even comes to broad-shouldered lady executives; that war is an heroic and virtually bloodless activity; that fame and success can be achieved indiscriminately by chorus girls, scientists, football players, and artists. To our edification, they show us how we felt about marriage in the twenties, crime in the thirties, war in the forties, big business in the fifties, and youth in the sixties. (Presumably future filmgoers will know how we felt about sex in the seventies.)

As an influential art, motion pictures are being studied and analyzed as never before by young filmgoers who are excited by the medium's past accomplishments and its even greater potential for the future. The rich body of films from *Intolerance* to *The Godfather;* the work of directors from Griffith to Kubrick; the uses of film for documenting events, ideas, and even emotions—these are the abundant materials from which film courses and film societies are being created across the country.

THE PICTORIAL TREASURY OF FILM STARS also draws on these materials, encompassing in a series of publications all the people, the trends, and the concepts that have contributed to motion pictures as nostalgia, as social history, and as art. The books in the series range as widely as the camera-eye can take us, from the distant past when artists with a vision of film's possibilities shaped a new form of expression, to the immediate future, when the medium may well undergo changes as innovative as the first primitive movements.

THE PICTORIAL TREASURY OF FILM STARS is a tribute to achievement: to the charismatic stars who linger in all our memories, and to the gifted people behind the cameras: the directors, the producers, the writers, the editors, the cameramen. It is also a salute to everyone who loves movies, forgives their failures, and acknowledges their shortcomings, who attends Bogart and Marx Brothers revivals and Ingmar Bergman retrospectives and festivals of forthcoming American and European films.

"The movies!" The cameras turn and the flickering images begin. And again we settle back to watch the screen, hoping to see a dream made real, an idea made palpable, or a promise fulfilled. On that unquenchable hope alone, the movies will endure.

ACKNOWLEDGMENTS

My thanks to the ever-helpful staff at the Theatre Collection of the New York Public Library for the Performing Arts. And thanks to Gene Andrewski, Movie Star News, and especially Jerry Vermilye, for the photographs.

A. B.

CONTENTS

JAMES CAGNEY

PROLOGUE

He was, critic Lincoln Kirstein observed as early as 1932, "the first definitely metropolitan figure to become national." With an accent most Americans had never heard and with the aggressiveness of a man hurling himself into a packed subway car moments before the doors close, James Francis Cagney, Jr. was the first New York street urchin to grab a piece of the American Dream. Kirstein was right on target—Cagney was a national hero. People would line up as faithfully to watch him in Pocatello, Baton Rouge, and Lansing, as they would at the Loews Delancey, blocks from his Lower East Side beginnings.

Not merely a national figure, James Cagney was a "Star," almost from the beginning of his movie career. And he rapidly became an archetype, a vital national resource, a personage to be emulated in dress, speech, and swagger. His films—good, bad or indifferent— were, and are, almost all worth watching for his very presence. Of all that matchless generation of movie actors and actresses who came of age in the 1930s, none brought as much sheer energy to the screen as Cagney. Running, grabbing, fighting, rearing back and stopping short, dancing, screaming: Cagney whirled through his parts with the assurance of a lightweight boxer defending his title for the twentieth time. His verbal delivery, endlessly parodied, made the tamest line seem charged with irony or malevolence. And such was the force of his screen persona that it is easy to overlook the intelligence and subtlety of his acting. Through *The Public Enemy, Taxi, Footlight Parade, Jimmy The Gent, G Men, Angels With Dirty Faces, City For Conquest, Yankee Doodle Dandy, White Heat, Love Me Or Leave Me, Mister Roberts,* and right up to his last film, *One, Two, Three,* Cagney created a truly irresistible series of characters. While some may feel that all his roles were variations on the same theme, each part he played, when examined today, seems perfectly crafted to the needs of its particular film.

That craft is hard to define, but its foundations were taste and intelligence. Cagney knew exactly how far he could take a particular character, knew the point at which his intense energy would start burning holes in the script. The result was that no matter how far Cagney went, he never upset the balance of a picture. That perfect story sense, combined with his incredible arsenal of facial and physical gestures, made him the compleat movie actor.

Yet Cagney's eyes could suddenly turn as cold and empty of love as those of a vengeful cop. Pity and hope could drain from them instantaneously, releasing a chill which froze the screen. Part of what made Cagney a great star was the simple fact that he could really scare you, and could scare you seconds after he had charmed you into buying him a second drink. The German director Max Reinhardt, who cast Cagney as Bottom in his misguided production of *A Midsummer Night's Dream* in 1935, was greatly excited by this quality, "a mysterious, dangerous, terrifying uncertainty that never allows an audience to relax." Reinhardt thought him "the best actor in Hollywood."

Cagney's body, compact and wiry, was perfectly attuned to the charming-frightening alternations in his character. Because the physique was not intimidating in itself, only the pure force of his anger could—and frequently did—turn it into a fighting machine. Audiences could see the hatred tighten every muscle at a moment's notice. And subside just as quickly. Cagney's body was also a great comic tool; he controlled it with the discipline of a silent screen funnyman. His takes, the frantic windmilling of his arms, the way he reared back to throw punches that were not to be, could all be harnessed into a flailing, double-time exercise in wasted motion. From the energy Cagney gives off in a comedy like *Jimmy The Gent*, for instance, in the objects picked up but never thrown, in the pantomimed fisticuffs and phones slammed on hooks, entire villages could be lit. And when all that power was put to truly violent use, it was time to hide under the seats. Here was a true madman.

Cagney's perfect control of body, face, and voice made him the compleat movie actor, one without whom the Warners films of the 1930s, with their emphasis on urban mayhem and farce, can scarcely be imagined. He created every role he acted in. Inevitably and irresistibly, the parts all became Cagney's. This was true of Humphrey Bogart; it was not true of so formidable an actor as Edward G. Robinson. Cagney's personality was too vivid for him to ever be a character actor. "Everything he does is *big*," said Orson Welles of Cagney, "and yet it's never for a moment unbelievable because it's real. He's a great movie actor."

Cagney is a very private man. There is no "authorized biography" or autobiography, as of yet. But from a limited number of interviews, studio "puff" pieces, and profiles, a few facts emerge as unmistakably true. Those familiar with *A Tree Grows In Brooklyn* will immediately recognize in Cagney's boyhood travails the same bittersweet elements of pride, ambition, and alcohol.

James Francis Cagney, Jr., the son of James Francis Cagney, was born on New York's Lower East Side on July 17, 1899. Warners publicists stubbornly pushed Cagney's birthdate into the twentieth century, five years later, but the truth wins out: the baby-faced killer of *The Public Enemy* was already thirty-two years old.

Cagney's family moved to Yorkville, on the upper east side of Manhattan, when the boy was a year old, but the change of scene was hardly a step up. East Seventy-ninth Street was a raucous neighborhood, a prototype of the brawling urban milieu Warners created in such films as *The Mayor of Hell* and *Angels With Dirty Faces*. Cagney remembers his playmates tossing bricks at policemen and at each other. It was exactly the kind of neighborhood you would imagine Cagney to have grown up in, one that bred

CHAPTER II

BREAKING IN

accomplished club fighters like Irish Patsy Klein and Eddie Fitzsimmons.

Cagney senior was a lovable and soft-hearted bartender, working at a joint called Comerford's, on First Avenue. For one year he ran his own saloon—into the ground. "He was a good Irish businessman," Cagney recalled wryly. He didn't earn much and what he did make was often lost on the horses. More tragically, Cagney's father drank more than his customers. "My father used to put it away," his son remembers, "but he was a quiet drinker. You never knew he had it in him except by the angle of his hat. He would always tip his hat a little over one eye." Quiet or not, the bottle slowly killed him. "Near the end of his life," Cagney told interviewer Pete Martin, "alcohol made him so sick, they'd wheel an ambulance up to the door and take him away to the hospital. It was rough to see that." Cagney's father was dead at forty-two. It was a searing experience. The actor rarely drank on-screen and never off-screen. But a bit of the elder Cagney remains, caught in his son's screen portrayals. One of Cagney's most characteristic gestures—the tap on the chin to show affection—was a direct and loving steal from the old man.

Cagney's mother, Carolyn, was in and out of hospitals for a gall bladder condition, but stubbornly kept the family together. Cagney recalled that his mother's "drive to get us an education was an obsession with her." Her flighty, romantic, and alcoholic husband could provide no example in the household, but her iron will kept her five children from falling by the wayside. When Jimmy thought of taking up boxing, she forbade it. His desire to become a commercial artist, however, she heartily encouraged. Cagney attended Stuyvesant High School and then entered Columbia College in 1918.

But Columbia was a pipe dream. Cagney had worked from age fourteen on, as a waiter, bouncer, package wrapper, library custodian, poolroom boy, newspaper office boy, and draftsman. Entering Columbia, he had to work even harder. With older brother Harry and younger brothers William and Edward, he worked at an upper West Side restaurant, located near the college. His college memories are those of the busboy watching the "swells" eat through the kitchen window: "I wasn't in on the fraternities, balls, proms, and stuff like that." When his father died in 1918, Cagney was nineteen and college was over. With brother Harry in medical school, Cagney deferred to him, dropped out of Columbia, and started working full time to help see Harry through. It is ironic to recall Cagney's Tommy Powers in *The Public Enemy,* sneering at his brother's nightschool studies and stuffing sawbucks into his mother's apron. The distance from the realities of Cagney's own life was vast.

Cagney had always acted in neighborhood theatricals and shows; he now decided to try the profession of show business on a full-time basis. An adept dancer, or at least clever enough to appear adept, Cagney made an inauspicious debut in drag, dressed as a damsel in a vaudeville revue called *Every Sailor.*

He reached Broadway for the first time in 1920, auditioning for a chorus spot in a show called *Pitter Patter.* He landed both the job and his future wife, Frances Willard Vernon, "Willie," a dancer in the show. When *Pitter Patter* fizzled out in 1920, after a fairly healthy run, Cagney rebounded to another chorus job in *Lew Fields' Ritz Girls!* Stepping in the line was amusing, but hardly enough to satisfy either Cagney's ambitions or his checkbook. After marrying Willie in 1922, he and his new bride went to Los Angeles, osten-

JAMES CAGNEY
A characteristic thirties pose

sibly to spend time with her mother. They got a thirty-five-dollar-a-month apartment in Los Angeles (no steal in 1922) and made the rounds of the studios, looking for acting work, extra work, any kind of work at all. They could not get past any gateman in Hollywood, and returned disconsolately to New York.

There wasn't much work in the city, either, so the Cagneys packed their valises again and hit the eastern vaudevillle circuit, doing an act called "Out of Town Papers." When they took the act down South, Dixie audiences couldn't understand a word Cagney was saying. His Dead End Kid elocution and laser-quick delivery roused Southern vaudeville aficionadoes to head for the rest rooms. Cagney recalls that the act laid not merely an egg, but "a seven tier wedding cake."

More tank towns ("the Cagney circuit," he called it), more failure, and the twosome headed back to New York. There Cagney scored his first success, in a 1925 production of Maxwell Anderson's *Outside Looking In*. He was even noticed by reviewers. "James Cagney," wrote the *New York Sun*, "does tidily as Little Red."

The triumph was short-lived. Cagney tried out for the lead in a Philip Dunning-George Abbott show called *Broadway* and lost out to Lee Tracy. (Tracy went to Hollywood and in a series of cocky, headstrong roles—as press agent, reporter, columnist—demonstrated an energy and skepticism similar to Cagney's. What Tracy lacked was Cagney's warmth.) Cagney stayed on as Tracy's understudy and then was picked to play the lead in a London production of the play, only to be fired before embarking on the transatlantic voyage.

Good parts in *Women Go On Forever*, *The Grand Street Follies of 1928* and *1929* and *Maggie The Magnificent* followed. The breakthrough occurred in 1930. Cagney and a young actress named Joan Blondell appeared in Marie Baumer's *Penny Arcade*, directed by William Keighley, who would direct Cagney in many Warners films. It resulted in a Warners contract for both Cagney and Blondell, but in an indirect manner, as Cagney tells it:

Sinners' Holiday, which was my first film was originally a play [Penny Arcade] that lasted only five weeks. Al Jolson bought it on spec and sold it to Warner Brothers and they shipped the body with it. Jolson suggested I play the part I had in the Broadway stage version.

Cagney's contract called for five hundred dollars a week, guaranteed for three weeks, plus train fare to California. Cagney got on the train and, like they say, never came back.

Warner Brothers was truly a film factory in 1930. Its sound stages were swarming with personnel from sunrise to dusk, and actors were frequently called upon to make three pictures at once. They had no choice. Being under contract to Warners meant doing whatever the studio told you. First with sound, Warners had capitalized on that novelty to the tune of a staggering seventeen million dollar profit in 1929. The Depression would start making its impact felt in 1930 and Warners' net receipts slid to a still hefty seven million, a breather before the eight million dollar loss the studio would sustain in 1931. But optimism, if guarded, still reigned in 1930 and Cagney was stepping onto the most vital lot in Hollywood. Warners averaged a motion picture every week!

In those days of contract players, Cagney and Blondell joined a growing Warners stock company whose faces would become the stuff of America's dreams over the next two decades: Humphrey Bogart, Bette Davis, Paul Muni, Pat O'Brien, Loretta Young, Edward G. Robinson, Ann Sheridan, Errol Flynn, and Dick Powell, along with a host of such familiar character actors as Guy Kibbee, Frank McHugh, George E. Stone, Glenda Farrell, Allen Jenkins and Aline

CHAPTER III

CAGNEY AT WARNERS

Sinners' Holiday (1930)
Doorway To Hell (1930)
The Millionaire (1931)
Other Men's Women (1931)
The Public Enemy (1931)
Smart Money (1931)
Blonde Crazy (1931)

MacMahon. Films were written to suit this gifted, volatile, and comic group of men and women, and a familiar Warners style began to emerge: acerbic, fast-paced, cynical, a little off-color, and finally, sentimental. Many of the screenwriters, perhaps most, had New York or Chicago backgrounds—as playwrights and newspaper reporters—and they brought to their work the sardonic, sour-faced, neurotic, and absurdist vibrations of the city room.

The setup was tailor-made for Cagney. It took him little time to establish that Cagney and Warner Brothers and the '30s were made for each other.

First on the agenda was the filming of *Penny Arcade,* luridly and misleadingly renamed *Sinners' Holiday* (1930) for the movie version. Its running time of fifty-five minutes qualified the picture as more of a lengthy short than a feature but it was long enough for Cagney to make an impression.

22

SINNERS' HOLIDAY (1930). With Lucille La Verne

The New York Times thought his performance "the most impressive acting" in the film. Cagney's original contract had run out after three weeks, as long as it took to make *Sinners' Holiday*, so Warners handed him another contract and a role in *Doorway To Hell* (1930), one of the endless number of gangster films that rolled off the assembly lines between 1930 and 1932. Lew Ayres starred, but Cagney caught the eye of scenarists Kubec Glasmon and John Bright, who had just finished the screen-play of *The Public Enemy*, a Chicago underworld epic based on Bright's story, "Beer and Blood."

Cagney remembers the casual beginning to the film that led to all the gold. "A part in a film called *The Public Enemy* was suggested to me. I said 'Fine.' I didn't even read the script. If anybody blew a whistle and said 'Act,' I acted." The script itself was far from unusual: the rise and fall of yet another gangster. Cagney was offered a supporting part.

He had meanwhile completed

THE MILLIONAIRE (1931). With George Arliss

two more films, *Other Men's Women* (1931), for director William Wellman, and a George Arliss vehicle called *The Millionaire* (1931). Wellman was set to direct *The Public Enemy* and had already cast Edward Woods to play the protagonist, Tommy Powers. Glasmon and Bright thought the part made for Cagney. After watching the first day's rushes, Wellman agreed. The three men marched across the lot to the office of Darryl Zanuck, Warners' "boy wonder" production head, and told him that Woods as Tommy and Cagney as his sidekick, Matt, was a mismatch. Zanuck grumbled. Warners had a tradition of nurturing its younger actors and Cagney only had three pictures under his belt. In addition, Woods was about to become the son-in-law of gossip columnist Louella Parsons, then a power in the movie colony. Wellman and the screenwriters were not impressed by Zanuck's arguments and neither, ultimately, was Zanuck. Cagney got the part.

More than enough has been written about *The Public Enemy*.

Too much, in fact. The scene in which Cagney puts Mae Clarke on the receiving end of a grapefruit, startling as it might have been in 1931, has received more scrutiny than the "Odessa Steps" sequence in Eisenstein's *Potemkin*. And it's hardly worth it; on screen, the moment is over before one can say "oh, *this* is the scene . . ." Besides which, Cagney was haunted by the scene for years, literally driven from restaurants by winking patrons who paid waiters to deliver half-grapefruits to his table.

But *The Public Enemy* provided Cagney with a near-perfect vehicle. In the tale of a wily young gangster's meteoric rise from the genteel poverty of his Irish neighborhood to the heights of Chicago bootlegging society, Cagney was afforded an opportunity to show off most of his wares. The gangster, as critic Robert Warshow

THE PUBLIC ENEMY (1931). With Jean Harlow and Edward Woods

THE PUBLIC ENEMY (1931). With Mae Clarke

observed, was the "man of the city" and urban guile and mother-wit were Cagney's stock in trade. Tommy Powers was resourceful and vicious, but the film allowed him little of the sweetness Cagney had in such abundance. "A human wolf," said critic Dwight Mac-Donald, "with the heartlessness and grace and innocence of an animal, as incapable of hypocrisy as of feeling."

Tommy is a hard case, one who can smile delightedly as he shoots down an old-time neighborhood con who begs him for mercy. He pushes around men and women with liberated abandon and goes on a truly ugly killing spree near the picture's end, before being gunned down himself and dumped on his mother's doorstep like the evening paper. The Cagney wit and grace are, of course, inevitable, but at its center his characterization of Tommy is ice cold. The "message" of the film was that poverty bred criminality. Tommy's iron-willed attempt to rise from the lace curtain dignity of home via bootlegging represents his only real shot at success. An older brother's steadfast devotion to education as a passport to better things receives Tommy's withering scorn. In 1931, that Depression-ridden year, the gun seemed a surer bet than the diploma.

Remembered now as a "classic,"

mainly for Cagney's startling debut as a star, *The Public Enemy*, when released, was regarded as workmanlike, but no *Little Caesar*. *The New York Times* reviewed it as "just another gangster film. Weaker than most in its story, stronger than most in its acting." In truth, the movie is no great shakes. Jean Harlow, portraying the inevitable blonde moll, paralyzes each scene she appears in and Edward Woods appears better suited to the role of a bored socialite than a hungry young tough. The film's pace is often sluggish, as was so often the case in the early years of sound, when directors and screenwriters became obsessed with dialogue and the camera lost the freedom it had acquired when microphones were absent.

But Jimmy Cagney had established himself. "It seems to me," said one critic of the time, "that Mr. Cagney is a rising young talking-picture actor to keep an eye on."

The star himself was of two

THE PUBLIC ENEMY (1931). With Edward Woods and Murray Kinnell

minds on the matter. On his first trip to New York following the success of *The Public Enemy*, he expressed doubts about the future, perhaps coy ones. "They come and they go," he said of movie stars. "Of course there's an exception now and then, but you can't count on that. Two more years and I'll be looking for a job on the stage again—maybe hoofing. What's the use of kidding myself."

He might have been dubious about the future, but he was sure enough of the present to insist upon a thousand dollar a week raise from Warners. And this introduces another side of Cagney —his fierce and determined independence from the studio, combined with the economic shrewdness of an investment banker. His frequent squabbles with the studio over the next decade revolved around two points: a recognition of his ever-increasing value to Warners, and a desire for greater freedom in picking his roles. After *The Public Enemy*, Cagney had a couple of bones to pick; he wanted more money and less of the annoying extra duties that went along with being a Warners "personality." He rankled at doing personal appearance tours and at the studio practice of forcing contract players to entertain at luncheons for visiting dignitaries.

The Public Enemy gave Cagney a sense of his potential boxoffice clout, so he asked his younger brother William to come West and take over his business affairs. Their initial contract demand, the first of many the Cagney brothers would make over the next two decades, was turned down by Warners. Cagney gathered his wife and headed back to New York.

He had in the meantime completed two more pictures, finished before *The Public Enemy* was released. One was another Glasmon and Bright screenplay, *Smart Money* (1931), directed by Alfred E. Green. Cagney was cast against Edward G. Robinson, of *Little Caesar* fame, and played second fiddle to Robinson's smooth gambler and womanizer, Nick Venizelos. *Smart Money* was well-reviewed, and the public was first made aware of Robinson's considerable flair for comedy. Cagney made his presence felt, but it was Robinson's picture.

Not so *Blonde Crazy* (1931), a film that marked a real breakthrough for Cagney. The Glasmon and Bright story gave Cagney a chance to play comedy and the top billing he received was not to be relinquished until the midfifties. Cagney played a crooked bellhop who, in cahoots with a crooked chambermaid (Joan Blondell),

SMART MONEY (1931). With Edward G. Robinson

SMART MONEY (1931). With Edward G. Robinson (center)

swindles various guests before being caught and imprisoned. The role demonstrated Cagney's sweet and comic side, and his ability to give comedy the same force and energy he gave melodrama. Critics took notice of his versatility.

And Cagney was sitting in New York, waiting for his raise.

The situation was unique in its time, comparable to recent instances of athletes holding out for salary boosts until halfway into the season. It just wasn't done, and Warners executives were angered and unhappy. Cagney and Bette Davis, more than any two stars, balked at the studio system as early as the '30s. Their reasons for intransigence were similar to the ones athletes give today; their employment represented a form of high-salaried slavery. They were cogs in the studio machinery, fitted into roles and pictures dictated from above.

Cagney stayed in New York for six months, reunited with his family and friends. The bravery and *chutzpah* of his holdout dazzles the mind; he was at the very start of his career, not really established, just a few steps from the oblivion he had so recently emerged from. Yet here he was, daring Warners and the movie industry to throw him out. It was a role taken from his funniest and most hard-boiled films—the cocky Irishman challenging the stuffed shirts. Meanwhile, *Smart Money* and *Blonde Crazy* were well received and Warners, sitting on a pile of scripts tailor-made for Cagney, got restive. The Academy Arbitration Board stepped in and worked out a settlement. Cagney was given a new contract, lifting his weekly pay check from $450 to $1,000. Cagney and Willie bid his family farewell and returned to Hollywood. His first holdout had ended. There would be others.

Cagney returned and embarked upon his first golden period, creating a succession of memorable characters in a series of funny and explosive films. It was a great and joyous era in the Cagney career.

BLONDE CRAZY (1931). With Joan Blondell

In this two-year period, Cagney had more fights with Warners—more walkouts, scream-outs, tear-ups, and reconciliations. And he never did better work. The breadth of his talent became more evident with each film, his timing sharpened to perfection, and he became a truly great movie actor, one who understood the limitless potential of the medium and grasped the meaning of the fact that the camera *moved.* He was never funnier, never quicker and, just as important, was never given better parts. Taken together, his films from 1932 to 1934 represent the quintessential Hollywood portrait of that flashy, brash, and hard-nosed world it pretended was the city. Cagney played boxers, hackies, "no-good" lawyers, sleazy photographers, show business impresarios, cons, and ex-cons —and did so with relish. "Cagney," said *New Theatre*, "is the perfect portrait of the American man-boy." His violence was at once "anarchic, ruthless, funny, and tender." Cagney brought to his parts a positively ferocious amount of energy, body English, good humor, bad grammar, and pure joy in conniving.

Cagney's excess adrenalin was put to good use by the incredible pace at Warners. "We did pictures like *Picture Snatcher* in fifteen

CHAPTER IV

THE FIRST GOLDEN PERIOD, 1932-1934

Taxi (1932)
The Crowd Roars (1932)
Winner Take All (1932)
Hard To Handle (1933)
Picture Snatcher (1933)
The Mayor Of Hell (1933)
Footlight Parade (1933)
Lady Killer (1933)
Jimmy The Gent (1934)

days," the star recalled in an interview. "And this is perhaps why people today think they move so fast." A story Cagney tells about Lloyd Bacon, director of *Picture Snatcher*, gives a good indication of the breakneck and haphazard way in which motion pictures were churned out in Burbank:

Lloyd Bacon actually shot rehearsals. [In a scene with Ralph Bellamy and Patricia Ellis] I heard the cue come and I walked through the door, went up to the desk and did the necessary. As I was working out what I was going to do for the scene and got all the business done I heard Bacon say 'Cut. Give me that one.' So I said I was rehearsing. He said 'Fine. Over there.' And we started on the next scene.°

°*Films and Filming*, March 1959.

TAXI (1932). With Loretta Young

Cagney's first picture upon returning was an excellent Glasmon and Bright comedy-drama called *Taxi*. Directed by Roy Del Ruth and co-starring Loretta Young, it was the first of many pictures in which Cagney acted in the style of an outlaw without actually being outside the law. He portrayed the leader of an independent group of taxi drivers who are trying to strike out against the entrenched taxi fleet owners. A fiery little portrait of the city, *Taxi* had a familiar roster of Warners supporting players, including George E. Stone, Guy Kibbee, David Landau, and a bit player named George Raft.

The scenario had Cagney avenging his brother's death by stalking the city, gun in hand, despite Young's attempts to stop him. The killer in Cagney was softened by Cagney's comic first screen discourse in Yiddish, breathless and larded with blarney. Once again, Glasmon and Bright's unerring gift for reproducing the feel of urban dialogue served Cagney well; their part in the launching of his screen rise can hardly be underestimated.

Taxi was one of the most lucrative of Cagney's early films, and a personal triumph. "We believe Cagney's popularity could equal or overtake that of Gable's this 1932," cooed the *New York Daily News*. "He has a grand sense of humor and he's one swell actor."

But his sense of humor was ill-served in his next film, *The Crowd Roars*. Those who have ridden in New York cabs may feel that this story of a racing driver was a logical sequel to *Taxi*, but its scenario was a lame second. Glasmon and Bright, collaborating with Niven Busch and Seton I. Miller, fumbled this one, even with Howard Hawks as director. Because of Hawks' well-deserved reputation, *The Crowd Roars* has received praise and a scrutiny it hardly merits. A competent Grade-B melodrama, it has little of the zest that made this first golden period of Cagney's filmmaking so appealing. While Cagney could do anything well, his role as an auto racer seemed written in the wrong key.

Ironically, the factors that made *The Crowd Roars* an inappropriate vessel for Cagney's gifts provide important clues as to the sources of the star's bonds with his audience.

Briefly, *The Crowd Roars* concerns Joe Greer, a successful racing driver who wants his younger brother Eddie (Eric Linden) to avoid the same career. Eddie persists and becomes a famous and successful practitioner of the sport, while Joe hits the skids

THE CROWD ROARS (1932). With Guy Kibbee, Frank McHugh, and Eric Linden

after causing a fatal accident at the track. He drinks, mopes around, and grows a stubble of beard while girl friend Lee (Ann Dvorak) tries to get him back on his feet. At the film's conclusion, Joe substitutes for the injured Eddie in a race, wins it, and the brothers are reunited.

So what's wrong? The role of a racing driver is basically that of a swashbuckler — goggles, scarf wrapped tightly around the neck, a multi-zippered leather jacket. One thinks of Douglas Fairbanks, Errol Flynn, Tyrone Power, maybe Clark Gable. Cagney was many

things, but he was not dashing. And he was not foolhardy. Driving a car around a track at high speeds, even for prize money, represented an abstract duel with death which did not fit Cagney's screen character. Death as the flip side of success in gangster films was understandable and even logical, but the criminal had gone beyond the law in order to survive, not to set records. And gangsterism was the most urban of professions; it was made to order for Cagney's style. But race driving was an unlikely career for a city boy to take; street-wise Cagney seemed too intelligent to wind up in goggles and a scarf. He was most attractive as a child of the streets, cutting as many corners as possible to stay alive in a hazardous world. That great characterization did not jibe with films such as *The Crowd Roars*. Contemporary reviews of the film were lukewarm.

With the above in mind, one can happily report that Cagney came back to the city in his next film, *Winner Take All*, playing a boxer named Jim Kane. Boxing was another logical option for a poor city boy; it meant getting one's fighting off the streets and into the marketplace. It was a way up and out, and a natural arena for Cagney, who grew up in a neighborhood of club fighters. (The ring would play a role in two other Cagney films, *The Irish In Us* and *City For Conquest*.)

Winner Take All was directed by Roy Del Ruth from a Robert Lord-Wilson Mizner script which made Cagney a broken-down fighter trying to recover his health on a western ranch. He falls for a country girl (Marian Nixon), returns to New York, resumes his ring career and falls into the clutches of a society girl (Virginia Bruce.) It was a fairly flimsy but very successful movie, successful enough for Cagney to demand yet another new contract from Warners. Warners predictably said no and the cocky new star again grabbed a transcontinental train going East. For the second time in a year and a half, Cagney was on strike.

His demands were pretty steep. With bonuses, Cagney's salary had reached $1400 per week. He now insisted on a $2400 a week raise and Warner Brothers, in April of 1932, suspended him.

In New York, Cagney told newspaper reporters that his position was firm; unless Warners acceded, he would quit movies and take up the study of medicine at Columbia, following in the footsteps of his older brother Harry. The blarney was thick enough to slice, but Cagney was apparently nerveless in negotiations. He stayed in New York for six months, not even caving in when the lead in a surefire comedy called *Blessed Event* was waved under his nose. The part was given to his old nemesis from *Broadway*, Lee Tracy.

Arbitration was again necessary and in October of 1932, Cagney returned to the fold. According to *Variety*, he was guaranteed $2,250 for 40 weeks, on top of which Warners promised him a share of the profits. The contract also contained "escalator" clauses which

WINNER TAKE ALL (1932). Jim Kane knocks out his opponent.

WINNER TAKE ALL (1932). With Virginia Bruce

HARD TO HANDLE (1933). With Ruth Donnelly and Mary Brian

would lift his weekly earnings to the Olympian regions of $4,500 by 1936. Cagney told reporters that his vow to enter medical school had been "a gag."

He returned to one of the most creative and fruitful periods of his career, churning out four comedies, a drama, and a musical in a little over a year. First came *Hard To Handle*. The Lord-Mizner script was a gem of New York cynicism, centering around the activities of one Lefty Merrill, a freelance promoter and fastbuck artist, who dreams up stunt after stunt to raise the elusive shekel. Director Mervyn LeRoy simply

let Cagney roam freely about the screen, and the star turned in a dervish-like performance as Merrill. Allen Jenkins played a cohort, but most notable support was given by that fine comedienne, Ruth Donnelly. When her daughter (Mary Brian) wins a Merrill-sponsored dance marathon and Merrill, naturally, cannot pay up in cash, she insists that he at least marry the girl. He does.

Hard To Handle amplified an important trend in the Cagney films of the '30s—one first noticeable in *Taxi*—and that is the placing of Cagney in roles which hedged on the star's position vis-

PICTURE SNATCHER (1933).
With Patricia Ellis

a-vis the law. While filmgoers invariably associate Cagney with underworld parts, the truth is that of all his starring roles in the early '30s, only Tommy Powers was a full-fledged gangster. He *did* regularly play either ex-cons or shysters, lovable rogues whose earnings, if not plainly illegal, were at best dubious. In the latter category are the glib promoter of *Hard To Handle* and the irrepressible, ambulance-chasing "lawyer" of *Jimmy The Gent.* Straddling both categories was the role of Danny Kean in *Picture Snatcher,* the Lloyd Bacon picture Cagney did after *Hard To Handle.* Kean is an ex-con hired by a scandal sheet to photograph celebrities at moments in which they preferred anonymity.

By giving Cagney such roles, Warners played the shrewdest of hunches—that audiences responded to Cagney as an outlaw, but wanted to see him live. Since movie gangsters had to die at picture's end, the way to allow Cagney to survive on screen was to give him roles in which his larcenous heart eschewed homicide. The killer instinct was muted and his pickpocket's agility was fully choreographed. Audiences were able to love him without guilt and without having to dread his bloody demise. (Cagney's band-

age-swathed wind-up in *The Public Enemy* was gruesome enough to last an entire career.) This careful switch in his screen character ultimately led to Cagney's being credible as an FBI agent in *G Men* (1935).

Picture Snatcher fit comfortably into this scheme. Ex-con Kean is hilarious and distasteful as he peeks through windows, surprises tuxedo-clad bigwigs as they exit nightclubs with the wrong girl or on all fours, and generally makes a nuisance of himself. Kean hits rock bottom when he sneaks into Sing-Sing, his former mailing address, and snaps a photo of an electrocution. Writers Allen Rivkin and P.J. Wolfson were harking back to the celebrated moment in the twenties when a *Daily News* photographer, camera strapped to his shin, stood in the death house and stealthily lifted his trouser leg as murderess Ruth Snyder was bathed in voltage. The resultant front page photo was a scandal; the edition was a sell-out. In *Picture Snatcher,* Kean redeems himself by taking the picture of a wanted criminal. The film got good reviews; Cagney got great ones. "He is," said the *New York Sun,* "an exceptionally resourceful performer."

Another critical factor must be kept in mind when assessing the success of such Cagney films as *Hard To Handle, Picture Snatcher, Footlight Parade,* and *Lady Killer;* they were released in the absolute depths of the Great Depression. In this context, Cagney's vitality and wit were a tonic. He seemed so alive and his resources seemed so inexhaustible; this in a period when so many had simply given up. Cagney's cockiness, jauntiness, and optimism recalled a national self-assurance which had been crippled by the shuttering of banks and businesses and the loss of work that had followed hard upon the stock market crash of 1929. In 1937, *The New Republic's* astute film critic, Otis Ferguson, recalled what Cagney's films of the early thirties had meant to the country:

> . . . seeing him you couldn't help feeling better about the state of the industry—or the state of the nation for that matter . . . This half-pint of an East Side Irish somehow managed to be a lot of what a typical American might be, nobody's fool and nobody's clever ape, quick and cocky but not too wise for his own business, frankly vulgar in the best sense, with the dignity of the genuine worn as easily as his skin.*

The New Republic, Oct. 13, 1937.

In the midst of all the comedy, Cagney turned in a melodrama called *The Mayor of Hell.* In the wake of the great critical and box-office success of *I Am A Fugitive From A Chain Gang,* Mervyn LeRoy's searing film about prison farm brutality, Warners planned *The Mayor of Hell* as the juvenile delinquency sequel to that story. Cagney starred as Patsy Gargan, a grafter who gets appointed to a soft political job at a reform school. Once there, his heart is predictably softened by the appalling conditions at the school, where the boys (played by such as Frankie Darro and Farina) are badly fed and regularly beaten. Patsy goes after the source of the mistreatment, a sadist and shyster named Thompson (Dudley Digges) who runs the school. The boys hate Thompson enough to kill him during a riot, but their revolt is assuaged by promises of "reform" at the reform school, a typically pat and unsatisfying ending in the tradition of most Warners films that dealt with social ills. Gargan's relationship with the kids (they are open-mouthed with admiration; he is both tough and avuncular) was a kind of dry run for *Angels With Dirty Faces,* in which Cagney's relationship with the Dead End Kids was developed to the point of great art. *The*

THE MAYOR OF HELL (1933). With Frankie Darro and Madge Evans

THE MAYOR OF HELL (1933). With Madge Evans (left)

FOOTLIGHT PARADE (1933). With (left to right) Ruby Keeler,
Joan Blondell, Frank McHugh, and Dick Powell

Mayor of Hell was remade into *Crime School* in 1938, the Gargan character was transformed into a social worker (Humphrey Bogart) and the results were even worse.

Cagney must have been relieved to get back into his dancing shoes again, in his next film, *Footlight Parade*. This was the third major musical released by Warners in 1933. The company's losses had reached fifteen million dollars in 1932 and the musicals—*42nd Street*, *Gold Diggers of 1933*, and *Footlight Parade*— represented a lavish gamble to turn the financial

graphs around. The gamble worked. *Gold Diggers* and *42nd Street* placed second and third in *Motion Picture Herald's* list of 1933's most successful boxoffice films.

The production numbers mounted by dance director Busby Berkeley have been dissected and giggled over more than enough. Often overlooked are the tight scripts and snappy dialogue of the musicals, and *Footlight Parade*, directed by Lloyd Bacon from a Manuel Seff-James Seymour screenplay, is one of the best. As Chester Kent, a harried dynamo of a director, Cagney turned in a funny and razzle-dazzle performance. Such was Cagney's screen presence that he manages to dominate the proceedings even amidst the acres of legs, bosoms, and perfect teeth that Bacon and Berkeley engulfed the screen with. And Cagney had plenty of assistance, surrounded with the best of Warners' character players: Joan Blondell, Frank McHugh, Guy Kibbee, Ruth Donnelly, and Hugh Herbert, not to mention Dick Powell and Ruby Keeler.

The plot? A less than unique twist—the leading man in Kent's show gets drunk and can't go on —gives Cagney a chance to hoof through the massive "Shanghai Lil" number with Ruby Keeler. The number and the show are a big success, ending with the chorines holding flash cards which turn into Franklin Roosevelt and the Blue Eagle of the National Recovery Administration. *Footlight Parade* was, and is, a great deal of fun.

For sheer fun, however, one has to do a good deal of searching before uncovering two more explosively hilarious films than *Lady Killer* and *Jimmy The Gent*. Made consecutively, they represent the most successful use ever made of Cagney's dazzling comic talents. There might have been more

44

FOOTLIGHT PARADE (1933). With Ruby Keeler and Joan Blondell

virtuoso acting roles in Cagney's career, but none funnier than these two. They were nonstop, nasty, and downright funky. Never did Cagney seem more like a wild man, like a city animal loosed upon the civilized world.

Ben Markson's script for *Lady Killer* was cleverly served by director Roy Del Ruth. Cagney was picked to play the lead, a racketeer turned movie star. And implicit in the selection of Cagney was the canny intuition that American moviegoers believed he really *was* a racketeer turned movie star. Cagney's performance—the highest and purest camp—indicates that he shared this insight. So the film goes beyond being a comedy about Hollywood and becomes a subtle and even unsettling parody of Cagney's career. It created an outrageous biography for the star, but correctly measured his impact on the movie colony. For Cagney came across so totally as the child of teeming Yorkville that his stardom was a kind of cruel joke on the Rudolph Valentinos and John Gilberts who had inhabited the silver screen's ethereal Baghdad during the twenties. Suddenly Cagney (and Robinson and Blondell) had come storming onto the scene, spouting dialogue from the cityroom and the poolroom, taking movies out of the desert sands and high seas and into the streets of New York. Cagney, the prime culprit, was so raw that audiences half-believed he had slapped Jack Warner around to gain access to the screen. The palmy dream world of the twenties had given way, at least on the Warners lot, to a "realism" which was still dream-like, but at least looked like the real thing.

Lady Killer exploited these facts brilliantly. Cagney's Dan Quigley is a New York mob leader who flees westward to escape the law. Winding up in Hollywood, he starts taking bit parts in films, both to earn some money and to blend into the landscape. The blending is less than precise; his first part is that of an Indian brave. Cagney in headdress and warpaint was a sight to behold, as was Cagney in the velvet outfits of costume dramas.

Quigley succeeds as a screen star by the same methods that brought him success in crime—shrewdness and dishonesty. He builds a "following" by writing his own fan mail, flooding the studio with adoring letters. It works; Quigley is made into a major star. At which point his old gang shows up with a plan to rob the homes of Hollywood luminaries. A nifty, if predictable, plot turn, it provides a delightful focus to the tor-

LADY KILLER (1933). With Mae Clarke

LADY KILLER (1933). With Mae Clarke

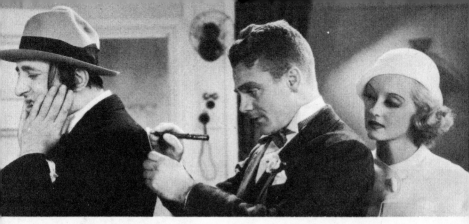

JIMMY THE GENT (1934). With Allen Jenkins and Bette Davis

ments of Quigley/Cagney's soul: is he a racketeer or a star? Or both? Favorably reviewed, the film managed to keep Cagney's image just a little bit clouded. Perhaps he really *was* a gangster.

The collaboration between Cagney and the temperamental Hungarian director Michael Curtiz was to prove most fruitful; *Yankee Doodle Dandy* and *Angels With Dirty Faces* emerged from their partnership. But the first script that brought them together, Bertram Milhauser's *Jimmy The Gent*, was the springboard for the funniest film of Cagney's career.

Cagney was ideal for the role of Jimmy Corrigan, a relentless squirt who hunts down the missing heirs to fortunes, taking a sizable chunk of the inheritance as his fee. Jimmy is not particular; if he cannot find the heir, he invents him. He thrives on disaster; front page headlines proclaiming air and road disasters which take the lives of the wealthy are his favorite reading. Jimmy is a jackal and the only lovable jackal in the history of movies.

Jimmy The Gent was graced by absolutely blistering dialogue and the central characters, without exception, were venal and abrasive. Bette Davis played the secretary to a rival and "high class" fortune hunter, played to perfection by Alan Dinehart. Allen Jenkins was Corrigan's punched-around assistant, and Alice White was a dumb blonde.

How dedicated Cagney was to the sleazy ambience of the picture was indicated when he arrived on the set for the first day's shooting wearing a crewcut that gave him the profile of a Boston terrier. From the back, he resembled Sluggo of the comic strip *Nancy*.

Curtiz was appalled but Cagney talked him into going along. The director had little choice.

Cagney gave Corrigan a personality to match his disfigured hairdo. Corrigan is not quite human; his relentless search for missing or nonexistent heirs has given him a perspective on the world not very different from that of a starving wolf. On top of his customary breathless delivery, Cagney blessed Corrigan with a Lower East Side accent even thicker than usual. The mangled accent, along with his butchered haircut and cash register brain, made him Cagney's most irresistibly repulsive creation.

Corrigan decides to put some class into his operation, tired of spending his days throwing furniture at Louie (Jenkins). Visiting the high-toned offices of his similarly larcenous opposition, Corrigan delicately sips his tea, cup after cup, and stares at the panelled walls, trying to figure out whether it's classy or absurd. Cagney's genius in *Jimmy The Gent* is to walk the line between the grotesqueness of his character's calling and manner and the essential lovability of the Lower East Side mug. Corrigan, against all odds, is more character than caricature.

Curtiz' direction helped immeasurably. In a wonderful scene, Corrigan goes after a missing heir named Joe Rector (Arthur Hohl), who just happens to be on the lam from the police. Corrigan discovers the brownstone where Rector is hiding and flushes him out by hiring men to pose as newshawks and parade up and down in front of the building barking out incomprehensible headlines containing the words "Joe Rector." An interior shot of Rector's hideout shows him alerted by the cries, straining to hear the headline, but maddeningly able only to hear "Rector" over and over. He leaves the building gingerly, a step at a time, beckoning the newshawks, who ignore him. Rector must go out on the street to purchase the bogus paper. When he scurries back inside to his apartment, Corrigan is sitting in an easy chair.

"If this *[Jimmy The Gent]* wasn't the fastest little whirlwind of true life on the raw fringe," wrote Otis Ferguson in 1937, "then I missed the other one." Like so many gems of the '30s, it has dropped from sight, rarely revived, and never shown on television. Not dated or quaint, *Jimmy The Gent* is simply a great American comedy. Its absence from circulation cheats us all.

After *Jimmy The Gent*, the uniformly high quality of Cagney's efforts showed a small decline, due to films that were either uninspired or misdirected. Not all fell in this category, of course. *Here Comes The Navy* was a first-rate comedy and *G Men,* Cagney's one real smash hit of the period, was a solid action-comedy-drama and a fascinating bit of history. *A Midsummer Night's Dream,* Warners' attempt at "High Art," was universally acknowledged to have been a mistake. Otherwise, Cagney was given roles that were predictable, had their share of laughs, but were just a little bit tired. Cagney began to feel it, too. Weary of being asked to go through the lovable tough guy paces again and again, he left Warners in 1936. After two lackluster years at Grand National, he returned to Warners and began another truly creative period.

In the summer of 1934, Cagney had one of his few brushes with notoriety. Sacramento police detective Ray Kunz, a member of California's subversive-hunting "Red Squad," claimed that Cagney had been mentioned in a letter written by Ella Winter, wife of "muckraking" author Lincoln Steffens, to Sacramento Communist Party official Caroline Decker. The letter implied that the star was a

CHAPTER V

A SLIGHT DIMOUT— 1934-1938

He Was Her Man (1934)
Here Comes The Navy (1934)
The St. Louis Kid (1934)
Devil Dogs Of The Air (1935)
G Men (1935)
The Irish In Us (1935)
A Midsummer Night's Dream (1935)
Frisco Kid (1935)
Ceiling Zero (1935)
Great Guy (1936)
Something To Sing About (1937)

contributor to the Party. Associated Press picked up the story and wired it across the country. Cagney's denial was immediate— he had a lot to lose:

I am proud to call myself a 100 percent American. This old country has been pretty good to me. It certainly would be ridiculous for me to align myself with any communistic, socialistic, Nazi, White Shirts, Silver Shirts or any other anti-American movement because I would be the first to suffer should these radical movements and agitations succeed.*

The story was over as soon as it started, although Cagney, like most people in Hollywood, would
New York Herald Tribune, August 18, 1934.

HE WAS HER MAN (1934). With Joan Blondell

HE WAS HER MAN (1934). With Bradley Page and Ralfe Harolde

have to face the House Committee on Un-American Activities a half-dozen years later and again proclaim his loyalty. But the Red Scare was a lot more interesting than Cagney's next movie, a bizarre Lloyd Bacon picture called *He Was Her Man*. The hectic Tom Buckingham-Niven Busch script had Cagney typed as a safecracker who takes off to Portugal with Joan Blondell, playing a retired prostitute in love with Victor Jory. American audiences were not fond of seeing much-loved actresses freely plying the oldest of professions. The movie took a short cut to oblivion.

A lot livelier was Bacon's *Here Comes The Navy*, which would be noteworthy if only for the fact that it marked the first of eight times that Cagney would appear with Pat O'Brien. The two men immediately demonstrated their matchless chemistry. The pattern was set in *Here Comes The Navy:* Cagney plays an independent, brawling rebel who goes AWOL and faces courtmartial, and O'Brien is his superior officer. O'Brien always had superior rank.

It made sense: Cagney played shanty Irish, O'Brien seemed to have moved up to the lace curtain class. Cagney was the club fighter and O'Brien the classy, stand-up counter-puncher. O'Brien's wit relied more on irony and side-of-the-mouth cynicism than Cagney's, which exercised the body as well as the brain; a punch in the mouth was never far away. But the two men shared a great natural warmth and rectitude; the friendship so obvious on screen was carried on off the screen, and the men became fast friends.

Here Comes The Navy was the first Cagney picture to receive an Academy Award nomination as Best Picture, put up as a sacrificial lamb in the year of Frank Capra's Oscar-sweeping *It Happened One Night*. A crisp film with the kind of tart dialogue that disappeared from screen comedies after the '30s, it too has disappeared from view.

Cagney finished out 1934 with *St. Louis Kid*, directed by Ray Enright from a Warren Duff-Seton I. Miller scenario, and *Devil Dogs of the Air*, a Lloyd Bacon picture written by Malcolm Stuart Boylan and Earl Baldwin. The former was a typical Warners picture about the Depression. Cagney plays a truck driver who gets involved in the farm revolt of the mid-thirties: disgruntled dairy farmers protesting plummeting prices by preventing truck drivers from delivering milk. The plot turns melodramatic, avoiding the social issues, and centering the movie on a hoked-up

HERE COMES THE NAVY (1934). With Frank McHugh and Pat O'Brien

HERE COMES THE NAVY (1934). With Gloria Stuart

THE ST. LOUIS KID (1934). With Allen Jenkins, Addison Richards, and Patricia Ellis

murder charge against Cagney. As *The New York Times* observed, "It is still worth a filmgoer's time to watch Mr. Cagney hang one on somebody's button, but somehow the spectacle seems less than epic after you have watched the film pussyfoot around an important subject." Warners was the only studio in Hollywood that touched on "topical" matters but after *I Am A Fugitive From A Chain Gang* and a bizarre 1933 William Wellman film called *Heroes For Sale*, it invariably clouded the social problems with gangsterism or contrived "solutions." *St. Louis Kid* was in that tradition.

Devil Dogs of the Air, which concerned the Marine Flying

Corps, brought O'Brien and Cagney together again. And again it cast O'Brien as the officer and Cagney as the raw recruit; the former the mature and responsible Irishman who has put his fights behind him (but can, in a pinch, take care of himself), the latter a street brawler new to the discipline of the armed forces. As in *Here Comes The Navy*, Cagney learns his lesson the hard way, but emerges as a model flyer. He was now all set to join the Federal Bureau of Investigation.

Warner Brothers' publicists made much ado about *G Men*, a shoot-'em-up drama about the training of a young FBI agent. The mid-thirties had seen the rise of a cult of the FBI, an organization of infallible gangbusters who always got their man. The headlines about the capture of John Dillinger had been shrewdly orchestrated to benefit the Bureau, and director J. Edgar Hoover let few opportunities for publicity pass untouched. So when Cagney, who had traditionally played outlaws

DEVIL DOGS OF THE AIR (1935). With Helen Lowell and Margaret Lindsay

G MEN (1935). With Margaret Lindsay

G MEN (1935). With Ann Dvorak

or quasi-outlaws, took the part of Brick Davis, an unsuccessful lawyer who joins the FBI when a childhood buddy is gunned down by hoodlums, Warners heralded it as an important step in the fight against crime.

"'Public Enemy' Becomes Soldier of the Law," proclaimed the advertising copy. "Hollywood's Most Famous Bad Man Joins the G Men and Halts the March of Crime . . . The fact that Jimmy Cagney, the historic 'Public Enemy' of 1931, now plays the lead in this epic of the end of gangdom, makes its appeal infallible." Warners even claimed that the film itself would slow the spread of crime.

Whatever the pitch, it worked. Released in the summer of 1935, *G Men* was one of the most lucrative films Cagney made during the thirties. Whether it was curiosity to see Cagney play a "soldier of

THE IRISH IN US (1935). With Frank McHugh, Mary Gordon,
Olivia de Havilland, and Pat O'Brien

the law" or just the general appeal of a solid action film, or even the media appeal of the FBI in those days of heroic, front-page outlaw hunts, *G Men* packed them in. William Keighley, who had last directed Cagney on Broadway in *Penny Arcade,* made good use of Seton I. Miller's script and balanced the scenes depicting the scientific "crimestopping" of the Bureau (fingerprint file, ballistics lab) with blistering shoot-outs. Cagney was terrific, throwing all his outlaw energy on the side of the law and becoming a valuable tool of the federal government. A lively film, *G Men* received raves of such magnitude that one won-

ders if reviewers expected that a pan would result in midnight knocks on their doors. Robert Armstrong, the man who brought King Kong into captivity, performs admirably as Cagney's superior at the Bureau, including perhaps the most obnoxious laughing scene in movies, during Cagney's karate lesson. Ann Dvorak, Margaret Lindsay, and Barton MacLane do predictable, competent turns.

After doing a negligible little Lloyd Bacon film called *The Irish In Us* (with O'Brien, of course), Cagney got trapped in Great Art. Warners had imported the famous German stage director Max Reinhardt to put some class into the

THE IRISH IN US (1935). With Pat O'Brien and Olivia de Havilland

operation, and Reinhardt decided to cast a virtually all-star roster of Warners contract players in *A Midsummer Night's Dream:* Cagney as Bottom, Dick Powell as Lysander, Mickey Rooney as Puck, Jean Muir as Helena, Joe E. Brown as Flute, Hugh Herbert as Snout, Victor Jory as Oberon, and Frank McHugh as Quince. Reinhardt could not get over Cagney; he was "the best actor in Hollywood . . . few artists have ever had his intensity, his dramatic drive. Every movement of his body, and his incredible hands, contributes to the story he is trying to tell."

Reinhardt was correct, but the casting was still wrong. Cagney was more Puck than Bottom, whom Shakespeare had given the "intensity" of a rock. No one could believe Cagney as the stolid dumbbell of a weaver and critical praise went primarily to Rooney and Brown. Cagney wanted more variety in his roles but *A Midsummer Night's Dream* was not a happy occasion for him. After two more films he would leave Warn-

A MIDSUMMER NIGHT'S DREAM (1935). With Hugh Herbert and Joe E. Brown

A MIDSUMMER NIGHT'S DREAM (1935). With his fellow artisans

A MIDSUMMER NIGHT'S DREAM (1935). As Bottom

FRISCO KID (1935). With Margaret Lindsay

ers again, this time actually jumping to another company.

He first completed *Frisco Kid* for Lloyd Bacon. A tale of the Barbary Coast days of the late nineteenth century, the Warren Duff-Seton I. Miller script gave Cagney a lot of brawling to do, but the film's timing could not have been worse. Samuel Goldwyn's production of *Barbary Coast* had been released just months before, a lavish spectacle directed by Howard Hawks, with a script by no less than Ben Hecht and Charles MacArthur. Hawks' cast —Edward G. Robinson, Miriam Hopkins, Joel McCrea, Walter Brennan, Frank Craven, and Brian Donlevy—proved to be an act that Cagney, Margaret Lindsay, and Ricardo Cortez could hardly be expected to follow. *Frisco Kid* never emerged from the shadow of *Barbary Coast*. Cagney was getting restless.

Ironically, his last picture for Warners, *Ceiling Zero*, was di-

FRISCO KID (1935). With Lily Damita and Ricardo Cortez

rected by Hawks. Cagney again played an undisciplined aviator and O'Brien was again his responsible superior. Both men might have been getting weary of such roles, but audiences apparently weren't; *Ceiling Zero* was well reviewed and well attended, perhaps as much for Hawks' skillfully directed flying scenes as for Cagney and O'Brien's typically gritty performances.

Warners had some more racketeering scripts ready for Cagney, who was now receiving forty-five hundred dollars a week. Only he could have walked away from such a contract. But Cagney's law-yers searched for an excuse to break the Warners pact and found it when they discovered that the studio had permitted Cagney to receive second billing to O'Brien on *Ceiling Zero*, in violation of its agreement with the star. Cagney also claimed that he had been called upon to make five pictures a year, another alleged violation of his contract. He walked out.

Surprisingly, he did not join up with another major studio, sought after as he was. No major company of those days would have granted Cagney the independence he desired. Studios were autocracies, ruled over by men who controlled the making of movies at every step of the way—men like Louis B. Mayer and Irving Thalberg at MGM, Harry Cohn at Columbia, David O. Selznick at RKO, and, of course, the brothers Warner. So Cagney signed with Grand National Pictures, a new company that had been formed out of the wreckage of the old Pathe company. Grand National guaranteed him one hundred thousand dollars per picture, plus a cut of the profits. But the litigation went on and on; it was one year between the release of *Ceiling Zero* and his first film for Grand National, *Great Guy*.

The wait wasn't worth it. Cagney's "independence" at Grand National resulted in nothing spectacular. While Cagney had told interviewers he wanted to get away from typecasting and prove his abilities in serious drama, citing the works of Synge and O'Casey as possible avenues for his talents, the two pictures he made for Grand National provided no such breakthroughs. Both pictures were typically taut and funny, but either of them could

CEILING ZERO (1935). With June Travis and Pat O'Brien

GREAT GUY (1936). With Edward Gargan and Mae Clarke

have been turned out at Warners.

In *Great Guy*, directed by John G. Blystone, Cagney was paired with his old partner in grapefruit, Mae Clarke, and given the not unusual role of an ex-prizefighter, Johnny Cave, turned deputy inspector for the Bureau of Weights and Measures. The standard thirties plot involved his efforts to trap a gang of shysters prone to short-weighting customers. Johnny hoists the crooks by their own petard, using methods of dubious legality to bring them to justice. Critics generally enjoyed the film,

and welcomed Cagney's return, but wondered why he had gone away if only to return in *Great Guy*, really only a cheaper-looking remake of roles he had turned in time and again for Warners.

Cagney shrewdly tried a change of pace for his next (and last) picture for Grand National. *Something To Sing About* represented another try at a musical, one a good deal less lavish than *Footlight Parade*. The Austin Parker script was a trim little satire of Hollywood, in which bandleader Terry Rooney goes West to make a

66

SOMETHING TO SING ABOUT (1937). With Mona Barrie

SOMETHING TO SING ABOUT (1937). With Evelyn Daw

musical. The film featured an amusing performance by William Frawley as a press agent and Cagney got a chance to dance again, but the satiric edge of *Something To Sing About*, while overpraised by so insightful a critic as Otis Ferguson, was considerably less sharp than that of *Boy Meets Girl*, the comedy Cagney made next. He made *Boy Meets Girl* for the studio he signed with after leaving Grand National in 1937. That studio was Warner Brothers.

Warner Brothers? Apparently convinced that a small operation could no better serve his interests than a film factory like Warners, Cagney again opted for the assembly line. And the pay wasn't bad; Warners bettered Grand National's deal, upping Cagney's fee per picture to a mind-boggling one hundred fifty thousand dollars. This was in an era of low taxation. Cagney agreed to work exclusively for Warners for five years. During this time he turned out twelve films. Among them were his very best.

This arbitrary "golden period" contains its share of duds and mistakes and is probably less consistent than the delirious period between 1932 and 1934, when the energy level of Cagney's work was enough to make the head spin. The great films of this period, with the exception of *Boy Meets Girl*, are mellower and gentler, even those of the gangster variety, like *Angels With Dirty Faces* and *The Roaring Twenties*. Raoul Walsh's *The Strawberry Blonde* is probably the best "gay nineties" film ever made, a lovely evocation of the late nineteenth century which avoided sappiness and oversimplification and gave Cagney the opportunity to turn in a stunning and graceful performance. *City For Conquest* is a classic soap opera of a fighter who loses his eyesight. The period ended with Cagney's Academy Award-winning performance as George M. Cohan in *Yankee Doodle Dandy*. Obviously, this is a very rich period to investigate. The razor wit and frenetic pace of the earlier period are missing, but the shadings and colorings of his characterizations in the 1938-1942 period are a delight to behold.

To start with an exception, *Boy Meets Girl* was a throwback to the early thirties. This can be attributed mainly to the fact that it

CHAPTER VI

THE SECOND GOLDEN PERIOD, 1938-1942

Boy Meets Girl (1938)
Angels With Dirty Faces (1938)
The Oklahoma Kid (1939)
Each Dawn I Die (1939)
The Roaring Twenties (1939)
The Fighting 69th (1940)
Torrid Zone (1940)
City For Conquest (1941)
The Strawberry Blonde (1941)
The Bride Came C.O.D. (1941)
Captains Of The Clouds (1942)
Yankee Doodle Dandy (1942)

was adapted from a Broadway hit of 1935, a year in which the anarchic and half-cocked perspective of Depression comedy was still operative in the theatre. Sam and Bella Spewack adapted their stage play to the screen and the competent Lloyd Bacon let the action flow

Boy Meets Girl is one of the two great satires of the picture industry released during the thirties, the other being *Once In A Lifetime*, the George S. Kaufman-Moss Hart play filmed by Universal in 1932. Both films, not unpredictably, made writers the heroes and studio heads and actors the buffoons, reflecting the aggressions of frustrated scenarists. And both films depicted daily life at a studio as containing the

BOY MEETS GIRL (1938). With Marie Wilson and Pat O'Brien

less pleasing aspects of a circus and a lunatic asylum.

Cagney and Pat O'Brien portray a manic team of screenwriters named Benson and Law, the kind of men who explain a story idea by storming into the studio head's office, climbing all over his desk and acting out the entire picture. As *Time* noted: "*Boy Meets Girl* goes like a house afire when James Cagney and Pat O'Brien . . . are expounding their boy-girl theory of cinema, imitating two British guardsman, acting five parts at once in one of their screen plays, and generally giving the impression of being possessed of a legion of March hares."

Benson and Law take particular pleasure in badgering a dumb and self-centered cowboy star named Larry Toms, well played by Dick Foran, and in affectionately toying with a pregnant commissary waitress (Marie Wilson), whose offspring becomes an idolized infant movie star. Ralph Bellamy played C. Elliot Friday, the harassed studio head. The film lacked the mordant wit of the script Kaufman and Hart cooked up for *Once In A Lifetime,* but made up for its shortcomings by the great exuberance and superb performances of its stars. The chemistry of Cagney and O'Brien seemed to grow with each film.

Their next collaborative effort, following the success of *Boy Meets Girl*, was another happy occasion, *Angels With Dirty Faces*.

If there is one Cagney film to place in a time capsule, in order to understand his appeal and import, it just might be *Angels With Dirty Faces*. Not merely one of his truly virtuoso performances, the role of Rocky Sullivan is a kind of summation of the appeal of the gangster to American audiences in the thirties. A sensitive script by Warren Duff and John Wexley was beautifully directed by Michael Curtiz. It was Curtiz' not inconsiderable achievement to balance the performances of Cagney and the Dead End Kids (Gabriel Dell, Leo Gorcey, Huntz Hall, Billy Halop, Bernard Punsley, and Bobby Jordan). What could have degenerated into a mugging match between the city kids and the original City Kid was turned into a genuinely moving relationship between a trapped adult and trapped children.

The story involves two childhood partners in petty crime, Rocky Sullivan and Jerry Connelly (O'Brien), who have gone in very different directions. Rocky has turned from petty to grand larceny and Jerry has entered the priest-

ANGELS WITH DIRTY FACES (1938). With Ann Sheridan and Pat O'Brien

ANGELS WITH DIRTY FACES (1938). With George Bancroft and Humphrey Bogart

hood. The turning point? Rocky and Jerry are racing from a freight yard after stealing some pens. As they scale a fence, the cops grab Rocky but Jerry scrambles over the side to freedom. Rocky goes to the reform school and as every movie buff knows, when Warners got someone sent away to reform school, he was doomed to a life of crime.

Emerging from the reformatory, Rocky begins a predictable journey, a succession of heists, stick-ups, and jail sentences. *Angels With Dirty Faces* really begins with Rocky in mid-career, having left the pen following a five year rap taken for himself and lawyer James Frazier (Humphrey Bogart). Rocky returns to the old neighborhood and rents a room

ting them to shoot baskets rather than pool, "getting them off the streets and into the playground." He asks his old pal Rocky to help him. Rocky agrees. Deterring the Dead End Kids from crime while still engaging in it himself, trying to convince them of its evil while being a living example of its benefits, Rocky is a contradiction. He would be a banality were it not for Cagney's magical performance.

He brought all of his boyhood into the part. Greeting everybody with "Whadya hear, whadya say," Cagney was both loose and tense, his body wound up tight, winding down in the hitches of his shoulders and the twitches of his neck. Fooling with the Dead End Kids in their "clubhouse," a place he uses to hide his money, he inevitably spars with them, throwing open-handed punches, mugging, jabbing, beating them down with his hat. Rocky is a manchild, an eternal adolescent to whom time and crime have been both kind and ravaging. The only adult burden he seems to carry is the inevitability of his death. Rocky is *the* most lovable gangster in all of movies, Tommy Powers grown older and wiser, at home in his city environment because the game is over. Rocky is no longer on the rise or even really on the lam; even as he settles accounts, it

while he goes about the business of recovering a hundred thousand dollars owed him by Frazier. It is then that he meets up again with Jerry, now Father Connelly, and the former "girl in pigtails," Laury, who has grown up to be Ann Sheridan, the most beautiful of Cagney's leading ladies.

Father Jerry is engaged in socializing the Dead End Kids, get-

seems a game he is playing from a distance. Rocky seems most at home as a superannuated member of the Dead End Kids.

A thousand brilliant details of Cagney's performance spring to mind, but especially the manner in which he returns to his neighborhood. Rocky is not only a criminal, but an unsuccessful one, a man caught and sentenced time and again. Yet he retains his dignity without getting trapped in pathos. Rocky's reunion with Jerry is a case in point; Jerry is both happy and embarrassed to see Rocky, embarrassed not for himself but for Rocky's embarrassment. Yet Rocky's ebullience immediately sets him at his ease. When Rocky rents a room, Cagney transforms this minor business into something quite stunning by neither treating the room as a step down or a hideout, nor by indulging himself in any of the hundred cliche mannerisms he could have gotten away with, like giving the room the "once over" and then whipping out a wad of bills. He takes the whole situation for what it is, maybe a way station or maybe the last stop. We are not sure. Neither is he.

In Rocky's relationship with the Dead End Kids, Cagney manages to achieve the highest moments in all of Warners' attempts to depict the realities of city life. Horsing around, sending the boys out for delicatessen, refereeing their basketball game, Rocky clearly reveals his bonds with the boys— the high good humor and shared misery of people getting the wrong end of the stick. So when Rocky goes to the electric chair, he performs the ultimate sacrifice by destroying those bonds. As a favor to Jerry he feigns cowardice so that the kids will be turned off and not see him as a model of behavior. The kids feel cheated and so does the audience. Whoever wanted to see Cagney cry?

Angels With Dirty Faces stands as a remarkable film, and Cagney's bravura performance resulted in his first "Best Actor" Oscar nomination, as well as the New York Film Critics award.

He then went from the sublime to the ridiculous.

It was inevitable, perhaps, that Warner would be unable to resist the idea of Cagney on horseback. And not merely Cagney, but Humphrey Bogart, too, by now only a couple of films away from top billing. The two were given chaps and ten gallon hats for a flimsy entry called *The Oklahoma Kid*, directed by the inevitable Lloyd Bacon, working on his ninth Cagney film in six years! Writers Warren Duff, Robert

THE OKLAHOMA KID (1939). With Rosemary Lane

Buckner, and Edward E. Paramore were given the task of making Cagney's cowboy debut believable. They tried the same tactic used to make Cagney's switch to the FBI credible in *G Men*—revenge. Brick Davis had joined the Bureau to avenge the death of an old friend; Jim Kincaid, the Oklahoma Kid, cleans up a town to avenge his father's unjust hanging.

Bogart was the heavy, of course, a man set on controlling the vice industry in Tulsa. He plays it straight, but nothing much helps.

Cagney sings "I Don't Want To Play In Your Yard," a song interrupted by gunfire, and also croons "Rockabye Baby" in Spanish, to a baby. Even in 1939, the film was perceived as camp: "Mr. Cagney is on a horse at the Strand," wrote Frank Nugent of *The New York Times*. "It is almost the only thing that distinguishes this picture from any one of five past Cagney films . . . . He cheerfully pranks through every outrageous assignment his script writers and director have given him . . . . He's just enjoying himself." Maybe, but

Cagney did not make another Western until 1955.

When Warners realized that James Cagney was not Hopalong Cassidy, nor was meant to be, the studio went back to form and cast him in two successive gangster pictures: *Each Dawn I Die,* directed by William Keighley, and *The Roaring Twenties,* Raoul Walsh's look at Prohibition. The first picture was a potboiler concerning a newspaper man framed on a manslaughter rap for getting too nosy about corruption in the District Attorney's office. The story contained a bewildering series of double crosses and escape attempts, but was well cast: George Raft co-starred, George Bancroft played the warden, and "Slapsy" Maxie Rosenbloom was a friendly jailbird. Cagney and Raft were as good as could be expected, but *Each Dawn I Die* was a tired movie.

And so was *The Roaring Twenties.* In the years since 1939, the film has acquired an undeserved luster, due to the fully deserved reputation of director Walsh, responsible for such great movies as *The Strawberry Blonde, High Sierra,* and *White Heat.* The script was written by Jerry Wald, Robert Rossen, and Richard Macaulay, from a story by playwright Mark Hellinger. Those heavyweights,

added to Walsh, and stars Cagney and Bogart, lay a burden of expectation on the film which *The Roaring Twenties* simply does not fulfill. An attempt at a summation of the gang film, the picture's self-consciousness as a kind of combination underworld film and "March of Time" documentary keeps it from really jelling.

Cagney plays Eddie Bartlett, a doughboy in the Great War, who returns home to find that jobs are hard to come by. Eddie gets a job

EACH DAWN I DIE (1939). With Jane Bryan and George Bancroft

as a cab driver and, with much sonorous narration concerning Prohibition and the rackets, phases into bootleging, getting involved with a coldly ambitious army buddy, played by Bogart.

Predictable shoot-outs and night club goings-on follow: men in tuxedos pushing blondes around various art deco hotspots. Eddie pushes the singing career of his girlfriend Jean (Priscilla Lane), but she gives him up to marry his lawyer (Jeffrey Lynn). Then more "voice of doom" narration accompanies Wall Street Crash footage (ticker tapes gone berserk) and we discover that Eddie is wiped out. Legalized beer seals his fate and he goes back to driving a cab. In a sentimental climax, he sacrifices his life to save Jean's husband, now a crusading prosecutor, from assassination by his vicious ex-friend, Bogart.

The Roaring Twenties was meant to be a kind of memoir. Bootlegging and stock market

THE ROARING TWENTIES (1939). With Humphrey Bogart

wobbles struck few nerves in 1939 and had none of the topicality with which Warners had successfully infused their action pictures. (*Confessions of A Nazi Spy*, also released in 1939, was more to the point.) *G Men, The Public Enemy*, even *Angels With Dirty Faces*, had flirted with current "issues," but the gangsters of *The Roaring Twenties* didn't have much to do with anything, and no one knew that better than Cagney. He was sick to death of gangster films and would let a full decade pass before making another one.

In 1940, "topical" meant war. Cagney tackled the subject in two radically different ways. He did a film called *The Fighting 69th*, directed by William Keighley, and performed in a network radio dramatization of Dalton Trumbo's antiwar novel, *Johnny Got His Gun*. The film depicted war as character-building, the r a d i o broadcast saw it as body-destroying. That Cagney performed in both with equal skill is eloquent testimony to his willingness to experiment, to extend himself in diverse ways.

THE ROARING TWENTIES (1939).
With Gladys George

THE FIGHTING 69TH (1940). As Pvt. Jerry Plunkett

The Fighting 69th, one of 1940s most popular films, was the very Irish-tinged story of a notoriously tough World War I regiment. As rebellious Jerry Plunkett, Cagney repeated a character he had already done, in *Here Comes The Navy* and *Devil Dogs of the Air*: the scoffer who gradually gets brought down to size and becomes a model soldier (or sailor, or pilot.) Glorifying the old-fashioned values of honor, duty and country, *The Fighting 69th* was clearly the product of a country which found itself getting closer and closer to involvement in yet another war. But no picture could be overly preachy with Cagney, Pat O'Brien, and Frank McHugh.

For Cagney, the role of Plunkett was one of the most unsympathetic he had ever assumed. Less a comical rebel than *Here Comes The Navy's* Chesty O'Connor, Plunkett is a vicious loudmouth who is all bravado at the training camp and cowardice at the front. His cowardice results in a rout of his unit, but he later gives up his life in an heroic action. The Boys Clubs of America voted the film their favorite of the year and Cagney their favorite actor. Errol Flynn and Mickey Rooney were second and third. Orson Welles received one vote.

Johnny Got His Gun was the flip side of *The Fighting 69th*, the ghastly story of the logical limits of heroism. Cagney played the title role, that of an armless, legless, and faceless being, mangled in combat, who is still able to think and articulate the buzz and swarm of his feelings and impressions. Radio listeners, hearing that familiar and vibrant voice as a creature of tubes and bottles, were shocked. The broadcast caused a furor and one of its less pleasant side effects was a summons issued Cagney to appear before Martin Dies and his House Committee On Un-American Activities. The Communist scare of 1934, which had brought a prompt denial from the star, was still operative, and Cagney, a soft touch, had contributed money in the years since to a variety of organizations the Committee felt were tainted. Cagney appeared, again avowed his loyalty, and was again cleared.

The author of *Johnny Got His Gun* was not so lucky. One of the "Hollywood Ten," Trumbo appeared before the Committee in 1947 and found himself imprisoned.

Cagney's next performance, in *Torrid Zone*, was less than controversial. Directed by William Keighley, this steamy little film was set on a South American plantation. It starred Cagney as a plantation manager and Pat O'Brien, as usual, played his boss. Ann Sheridan, whose career was starting to take off, got the movie's best reviews and deservedly so. O'Brien was nobody's idea of a plantation owner, and Cagney ran around with an absurd pencil-thin mustache of the kind usually drawn on subway movie posters. It looked like it had landed, rather than grown, beneath his nose. Luckily for Cagney, his next film was perfectly in character, and a melodrama in the grand style.

City For Conquest is, in its own way, almost as absurd as *Torrid Zone*. The plot can hardly be repeated with a straight face: a boxer goes blind after having an illegal toxic substance smeared into his eyes during a fight, but he goes on undaunted, selling newspapers so that his kid brother can go on composing. The film ends with the blinded newsie at the newstand, listening to his bro-

THE FIGHTING 69TH (1940).
With Pat O'Brien

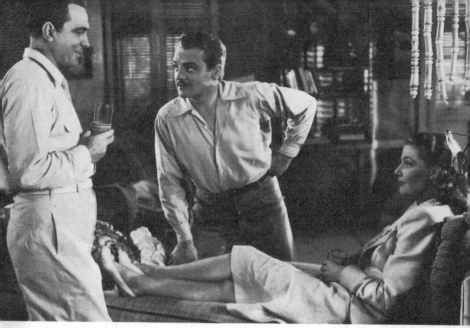

TORRID ZONE (1940). With Pat O'Brien and Ann Sheridan

TORRID ZONE (1940). With Ann Sheridan

*CITY FOR CONQUEST (1940). With Ann Sheridan,
Frank McHugh, and Anthony Quinn*

ther's symphony being performed at Carnegie Hall. But *City For Conquest*, under Anatole Litvak's direction, goes beyond soap opera and holds up as a genuinely moving film, lit by Cagney's magnificent performance, as well as the performances of Ann Sheridan, Frank McHugh, Arthur Kennedy, Frank Craven and Donald Crisp. Smaller parts were played by two young men named Anthony Quinn and Elia Kazan.

John Wexley's script was successful in allowing Cagney's sweetness to be evident, but not to dominate his character. It was a frequent mistake of scenarists in-

tent on showing the kindly side of movie tough guys to apply the sugar with a heavy hand. (Cagney's first independent feature, *Johnny Come Lately*, fell into this trap). But *City For Conquest*, an unabashed tear-jerker, used Cagney's toughness to make his fall from number one lightweight contender to blind helplessness all the more poignant. And the fact that his blindness was caused by the unscrupulous and sadistic application of a toxic to his opponent's gloves made the blood boil.

Cagney demonstrates the vulnerability of the fighter, Danny Kean, even before his mishap.

CITY FOR CONQUEST (1940). With Frank McHugh and Elia Kazan

When his gal Peg (Sheridan) goes off on a night club career (part of a dance team, her partner being a very greased-down Anthony Quinn), he is deeply stricken, jealous, wounded. The accident makes him feel useless; Cagney did not allow his renowned spunk to become mindless bravado or simple-minded optimism. Danny gropes around the apartment while brother Eddie (Arthur Kennedy) plays the piano, banging out the chords to his "symphony of a city." Danny, eyes almost closed, as if too modest to reveal his blindness, nods in pleasure as the music pours out. He likes it, likes it very much. It is a moment that only Warners was prepared to exploit fully: brother Eddie playing by a window opened to the teeming and humanity-choked streets of New York, while the blinded Danny, near-champion prize-fighter, says: "That's it." It is high hokum, the music striking chords down in the streets, the blinded boxer flashing in recognition of the meaning of the music.

Everybody loved *City For Conquest;* reviewers hailed the performances of Cagney and Sheridan, and marvelled over Warners' continued exploitation of city

THE STRAWBERRY BLONDE (1941). With Alan Hale

*THE STRAWBERRY BLONDE (1941). With Rita Hayworth,
Olivia de Havilland, and Jack Carson*

themes. Writing in *The New York Times*, Bosley Crowther declared: "Sometimes we wonder whether it wasn't really Warners who got New York from the Indians." This is one of Cagney's really fine moments on screen; to take a role so susceptible to soap opera and turn it into so personal and moving a characterization required the concentration of a great actor. That greatness was evident again in his next picture.

The outlook for *The Strawberry Blonde* wasn't really very bright despite the presence of Cagney, Olivia de Havilland (fresh from her triumph in *Gone With The Wind*), and a young beauty named Rita Hayworth. The film was based on a successful and somewhat saccharine play called *One Sunday Afternoon*, by James Hagan, which had already been turned into a movie, of the same name, by Paramount in 1933. Gary Cooper had played the young dentist, and the film had failed to attract much attention. But Warners shrewdly figured that the role of the dentist was better suited to Cagney's mercurial personality than to Cooper's shy diffidence, and decided to give the play another chance. Julius and Philip Epstein, Warners' resident writing brothers, prepared the screen play, and Raoul

Walsh was hired to direct. That Walsh was at the very peak of his powers is indicated by the fact that in 1941 he directed not only *The Strawberry Blonde* but *High Sierra*, which featured Humphrey Bogart's great performance as the aging outlaw, Roy "Mad Dog" Earle. The two films are radically different, yet each concerns the attempts of men to grow old gracefully and accept their limits. And each film was directed with enormous style.

Cagney was also at a peak in his career, a second peak. The first, in his *Jimmy The Gent* period, had been the perfection of a frantic, hilarious, abrasive characterization. The second peak saw the mellowings and understandings of middle age. Cagney, now forty-two, had just finished *City For Conquest* and was two films away from *Yankee Doodle Dandy*. He was avoiding the mistake of repeating his old roles, but also avoiding the mistake of drastically reshaping his image. He just got better and better. The word "delicacy" is not inappropriate in describing the added element in his acting.

That delicacy allowed *The Strawberry Blonde* to transcend its thin story involving the life and loves of a young dentist, Biff Grimes. Biff loses the hand of the neighborhood beauty, Virginia Brush (Hayworth), to an awkward but prosperous and crooked contractor named Hugo Barnstead (Jack Carson). Biff settles for the next best thing, Virginia's best friend, Amy (de Havilland). The not altogether credible plot has Biff used as a dupe in a scheme of Hugo's, ending with the dentist receiving a five-year jail sentence. When he emerges, Biff is movingly reunited with Amy. He settles down into an uncomplicated existence as a dentist, raising a brood with Amy. The turn of plot brings Hugo unknowingly into Biff's office, seeking emergency dental work. Biff ponders putting Hugo away for good with an overdose of gas, but decides against it. He sees Virginia again, still gorgeous but lacking Amy's warmth and humanity—and decides that he, after all, got the better break in life.

Despite the slender story, *The Strawberry Blonde* is a thoroughly engrossing film. One is hardly aware of its slightness while watching it, so easily does the film flow, and so beautifully scaled are the performances. Even the melodramatic prison sentence can't jar the balance of this picture, which hinges on the dentist's peaceful acceptance of his particular stake in society. The "gay nineties" aspects are never allowed to impinge upon the story. They provide a setting, that's all; *The Strawberry Blonde* is never "quaint." Olivia de Havilland's muted performance as the "second" girl turned "first" girl is lovely, and Rita Hayworth's beautiful blandness represented more inspired casting than virtuoso acting. She is gorgeous, unattainable, but ultimately not quite desirable and more than just a little boring. Jack Carson is excellent as the crafty yet klutzy Hugo, someone just a little too ridiculous to hate. The audience feels the ambiguity with Biff, finds it hard to muster up enough anger to root for the imagined homicide.

Cagney's last picture of 1941, *The Bride Came C.O.D.*, should have been avoided. The Epstein brothers' script, in conception and situation, was about ten years overripe, and there was little director William Keighley could do to help. Cagney as a scrappy pilot and Bette Davis as a willful society girl he "kidnaps" to thwart her elopement with a bandleader, were getting a little old for this kind of nonsense, which had been done a dozen times—and with a good deal more wit—in the thirties. But after *City For Conquest* and *The Strawberry Blonde*, Cagney was entitled to one bomb. Nineteen forty-one had been very

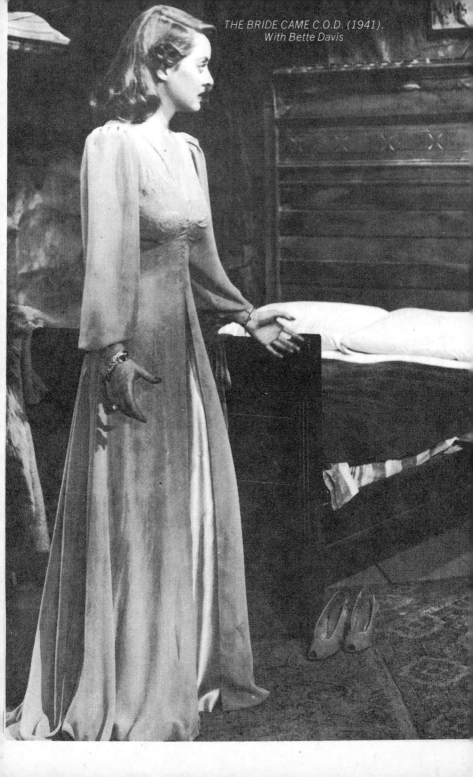

good for him, artistically and financially: his earnings for the year amounted to something over three hundred and fifty thousand dollars! As he faced the new year, with the country now at war, it was a sanguine Cagney who could relish the prospect of finally playing a sought-after role, that of George M. Cohan.

After completing *Captains of the Clouds*, a Michael Curtiz film about the Canadian Royal Air Force, in which Cagney played second fiddle to Technicolor (it was his first film in that medium), and to razzle-dazzle aerial photography, Cagney started preparing for *Yankee Doodle Dandy*.

The role of Cohan, with its singing, dancing and obvious theatricality, was a plum, but Cagney was the logical choice. Indeed, he was picked for the part by Cohan himself, who had retained final approval over casting after selling Warners the rights to his life story. Cagney's scrappiness, élan and versatility reminded the egotistical old hoofer of himself. The truth was that Cagney had reminded people of Cohan for a long time. As early as 1934, Howard Barnes, film critic of the *New York Herald-Tribune*, had written that "more than any other . . . actor . . . Mr. Cagney is the exponent of the school of acting of which George

M. Cohan is the brilliant dean. Eschewing histrionic fireworks he is adept at calculated understatement in which the slightest gesture . . . is extremely significant."

Cagney loved the part "because it was real American showbusiness" and it remains his personal favorite. Coincidentally or not, *Yankee Doodle Dandy* was his greatest boxoffice hit (a $6.5 million gross) and netted him his only Academy Award.

It *is* a bravura performance. Cagney mugs, sings and dances with energy and style. He caught more than a touch of Cohan's self-love, but managed to make the character a good deal more sympathetic than Cohan was in actuality. The film is more fantasy than biography, and Cagney understood that very well. And *Yankee Doodle Dandy* is more than biography; it is a kind of national anthem, a hymn to American heroism and drive. The Robert Buckner-Edmund Joseph script and Michael Curtiz' direction exploited every patriotic nuance. Released in 1942, a year in which the outcome of the war was still very much in doubt, the film operated on two levels. In its depiction of Cohan rousing World War One bond rallies, it operated as a World War Two bond rally.

The film's opening gives away

CAPTAINS OF THE CLOUDS (1942). With Dennis Morgan and Alan Hale

CAPTAINS OF THE CLOUDS (1942). With Dennis Morgan

YANKEE DOODLE DANDY (1942). With Frances Langford

its patriotic purposes. Cohan is called to Washington, by none other than President Roosevelt, to receive a medal. In the White House, Cohan proceeds to tell FDR his life story, as if the story itself is a national resource, a raw material of use to the war effort. Curtiz handled the White House scene less than gracefully: rather than get a Roosevelt look-alike, the director opted to shoot the scene from in back of the presidential desk. We see the rear of Roosevelt's head and the hint of rimless spectacles as he nods in pleasure at Cohan's tale.

After the stiff opening, Curtiz let out all the stops. Cagney is all over the screen, obviously happy with the material. He had worked on his dancing for months and it showed. The Cohan mannerisms he had mastered by watching the

YANKEE DOODLE DANDY (1942). With Joan Leslie

old master's only feature film, a 1932 Paramount curiosity called *The Phantom President.* The songs are all traditional showstoppers: "Give My Regards To Broadway," "You're A Grand Old Flag," and "Yankee Doodle Dandy." "When Johnny Comes Marching Home" was thrown in, as well as a chorus of blacks singing "The Battle Hymn of the Republic." The songs are woven into the story; the film does not stop for them. But that was made easy by the fact that so much of the story takes place on stage. Cohan's life was given over to his adoring public.

Besides Cagney, the film was well cast. Walter Huston played Cohan's vaudevillian father, Rosemary DeCamp his mother, and Joan Leslie was his sweetheart and wife. Family ties also

95

counted in the casting. Cagney's sister Jeanne, appropriately enough, played Cohan's sister Josie, while the role of Eddie Foy Sr., was attempted by Eddie Foy, Jr.

Given a full-dress premiere for the benefit of War Bonds, *Yankee Doodle Dandy* garnered enthusiastic reviews. It would have been nearly traitorous to pan the film but even taking that into account, the film deserved the raves. It holds up still as a solid movie musical, if a definitely old-fashioned bit of show biz hokum. Cagney may love the Cohan role above all others, but it allowed him none of the range of his greatest parts.

Yankee Doodle Dandy was a boxoffice bonanza for Warners, but Cagney's contract had run out again and this time there was no turning back. Cagney was determined to strike out on his own, turning a deaf ear to the studio's pleas for a renewal of his pact. In 1942, Cagney deserted Warners again, this time to form his own production company, under the banner of William Cagney Pictures, films to be independently produced but released exclusively through United Artists for a five-year period. Cagney's younger brother William, who had received Associate Producer credit on all of Cagney's pictures since *Torrid Zone,* had by now acquired a good deal of production expertise. His business acumen had already been demonstrated by the skill with which he had handled his older sibling's contract negotiations.

Movies should be entertaining, not blood baths," Cagney had said in the last days of his Warners contract. "I'm sick of carrying a gun and beating up women." But Cagney really had done little of that in the past few years. While he had been given his share of losers, he had also been given rich and sweeping parts, parts that had represented a new flowering of his screen personality. The roles had called for a degree of toughness, but certainly for none of the sadism of his early gangster period. Ironically, his most twisted bad guys lay before him, crazy men he would play in the late forties and early fifties. No, what Cagney was tired of was less the type casting than an inability to get opportunities for experimentation. The parts, even when great, were out of a certain pattern. He now felt he had done all the gangsters, mean or sensitive, and all the young men on the rise or wane, that he wanted to. He had told interviewers of his desire to do serious drama, even Irish drama, on the screen. Cagney felt, justifiably, that total freedom would not be his until he left Warners. Within the studio he could turn down roles but not purchase them himself; his choices were limited to properties Warners thought were viable and commercial. Wil-

ON HIS OWN

Johnny Come Lately (1943)
Blood On The Sun (1945)
13 Rue Madeleine (1946)
The Time Of Your Life (1948)

liam Cagney Productions would allow the star to develop his own properties and make his choices from all the available material on the literary market. He could do whatever he pleased.

Yet his greatest pictures were largely behind him. The irony is that Warners knew best.

It is not that Cagney made *bad* pictures on his own. Far from it. *Blood On The Sun*, for one, was a tight and suspenseful study of prewar Japan. And it is not that William Cagney Productions did not go out on limbs; it is doubtful, for instance, that William Saroyan's play, *The Time Of Your Life*, would have been purchased by Warners as a vehicle for Cagney. The major flaw in Cagney's attempt at independence was his failure to realize that stories about the city, whether contemporary or set in the 1890s, were the things he did best. Warners did not thrive in the thirties due to luck. The studio knew how to use its stars and concentrated heavily on an urban milieu that worked time

JOHNNY COME LATELY (1943). With Robert Barrat

and again. Within that milieu, Cagney had some marvelous parts.

But Cagney the independent wanted no part of urban pictures. And his very first effort, *Johnny Come Lately*, set in a small town of the late nineteenth century, was a try at cutting loose from that old Lower East Side image. The try was not successful.

Johnny Come Lately tried to burn too many of Cagney's bridges behind him. As Tom Richards, a hobo who helps an elderly lady newspaper publisher (G r a c e George) defeat the crooked interests who run her town, Cagney indulged himself in a heavy dose of whimsey. An occasional fistfight couldn't counteract the essential sappiness of the part, or the film.

John van Druten's adaption of the Louis Bromfield novel, *McLeod's Folly*, was so full of "lovable" characters—the vagrant, the sweet but righteous old lady, her faithful black maid, the drunken newsman, the town madam—that *Johnny Come Lately* never had a chance. A syrupy musical score added little to the proceedings.

Cagney, so tired of bullying women across the screen, made Tom into a veritable Eagle Scout. Audiences liked him better the old way. And *Johnny Come Lately*, directed by William Howard, suffered from what critic James Agee assessed as a "fatal commercial uneasiness." The first half of the picture is so gentle and good-natured that the Cagney brothers apparently feared it would lull audiences to sleep. The second half, filled with disorganized fights and crowd scenes, falls totally apart. While Agee praised the "general ambience of hope and pleasure about the production," he felt it lacked "cinematic judgment." Other critics were thrown off balance by the picture's lumbering pace, although much praise went to Miss George, a stage luminary here making her only appearance on film. No stampedes were recorded at the boxoffice.

So Cagney went back to the more familiar: a rough and tumble part as newspaperman Nick Condon, an American working in Tokyo during the twenties. *Blood On The Sun* was as hard as *Johnny Come Lately* had been soft and while the part of Condon was one-dimensional, it was a dimension Cagney could do better than anyone else. Released in 1945, the film was heavy on anti-Japanese propaganda but still managed to be an extremely skillful portrait of the long shadows cast by a country going totalitarian and militaristic. Condon, a newsman with Japanese friends who have been mysteriously murdered, finds the reasons behind the homicides to be linked to secret Japanese war

JOHNNY COME LATELY (1943). With (left to right)
Marjorie Lord, Margaret Hamilton, George Cleveland, and Grace George

BLOOD ON THE SUN (1945). With Sylvia Sidney

plans. One of the few Cagney films shown with any regularity on television, *Blood On The Sun* creaks a bit, but basically holds up well.

The intrigue theme worked so well that Cagney did it again, switching to the European front for *13 Rue Madeleine*, a Louis de Rochement production released by Twentieth Century Fox. (William Cagney Productions were tied exclusively to United Artists, so for the first time since 1940, Cagney's younger brother did not appear in the credits.)

13 Rue Madeleine, directed by Henry Hathaway (best known for Westerns like *From Hell To Texas* and *Rawhide*) was done in that quasi-documentary style so admired in Hollywood during the late thirties, forties, and early fif-

13 RUE MADELEINE (1946). With Walter Abel

13 RUE MADELEINE (1946). With Annabella

ties. Producer de Rochement was in fact responsible for the famous newsreel series, "March of Time," and had produced *House On 92nd Street*, a classic espionage film done in a documentary style. *13 Rue Madeleine* was the follow-up to that success and ran a close second in suspense and believability. Cagney, as espionage agent Bob Sharkey, has the difficult task of determining which of the American agents is in reality a Nazi agent. Realizing that plot machinations were foremost, Cagney played it very straight and very well.

After two action films, Cagney returned to experimentation. Not released until 1948, the Cagney Brothers' version of Saroyan's *The Time Of Your Life* was only Cagney's third movie in six years. This inactivity can be attributed to two basic causes: Cagney's desire to slow down the exhausting pace he set during the thirties, making three to five pictures each year, and his wartime activities.

Cagney's war effort included filmmaking and personal appearances. In 1944, he toured American bases in England and Scotland. Cagney sang, danced, and concluded his act, of course, with "Yankee Doodle Dandy." He also put in appearances at the Hollywood Canteen. The filmmaking consisted of two shorts for the Armed Forces: one dramatic, the other simply a narrative. *You, John Jones,* directed by Mervyn LeRoy and released in 1943, featured Cagney as an air raid warden describing what might happen if America was invaded by enemy forces. The film was considered one of the most effective released during the war, and co-starred Ann Sothern and Margaret O'Brien. *Battle Stations* was a 1944 Coast Guard documentary narrated by Cagney and Ginger Rogers.

But Cagney's decreasing screen activity had less to do with war than with an increased desire to get away from it all. He wanted to spend more time with Willie and with his adopted children, James, Jr. and Cathleen, and more time on his farms in Martha's Vineyard, Massachusetts, and Millbrook, New York. Never a member of Hollywood's fast set, Cagney, in his mid-forties, had begun the process of cashing in his chips. He certainly didn't need any money and his ego did not need pampering. For Cagney, acting had filled less a psychological need to be loved than an economic need to get paid. Cagney said as much in a reflective 1958 *Sight And Sound* interview: *

Sight and Sound, Winter, 1958.

THE TIME OF YOUR LIFE (1948). With Jeanne Cagney and William Bendix

I don't regard acting as anything sacred. When I went to Hollywood in 1930 I had to fill in a studio questionnaire. One of the questions it asked was 'How did you come to take up stage or screen work?' I gave my answer in two words: 'Needed job.' I never go to see my own films, not even the rushes. When they're finished, they're finished.

I went into show business strictly from hunger. Starvation helps to turn you into a pretty good actor, I guess.

By the late forties, Cagney was no longer hungry—in any of the possible senses of the word. The transition from actor to farmer had begun, a transition he would complete in a little more than a decade. He was becoming more an observer than a participant.

That change was reflected in *The Time Of Your Life*, novelist-playwright Saroyan's genial look at the patrons of a San Francisco saloon. A whimsical, generous play —a kind of good-hearted *The Iceman Cometh*—it had been purchased by Cagney Productions for 150,000 dollars. As Joe, Cagney was the observer, the wry and puckish commentator on the passing scene, the cockeyed optimist happy to see people nurture their illusions. The appeal of the role had a lot to do with Cagney's own maturation and need for a life filled with more of the basics than could be found in Beverly Hills. James Agee, who greatly preferred the stage version of *Time Of Your Life*, nonetheless felt that "those who made the picture have given it something very rare. It's obvious that they love the play and their work in it, and their affection and enjoyment are highly contagious." Indulgently directed by H. C. Potter and co-starring dancer Paul Draper, Broderick Crawford, Wayne Morris, William Bendix, and Jeanne Cagney, the film stirred little enthusiasm among moviegoers, but it was a highly personal statement for Cagney, who probably felt more kinship with Joe than with any of his other parts. Wry, generous, introspective; these qualities of Cagney were rarely depicted on screen.

The public, did, however, prefer another kind of Cagney. One, for instance, who was both a cold-blooded killer and a mother-obsessed mental case.

From the autumnal mellowness of *The Time Of Your Life*, Cagney turned back to blistering gangsterism, in the highstrung and audacious *White Heat*.

If Cagney was a free spirit, he was also a man with the shrewdest business sense in Hollywood. The Cagney Brothers' five-year deal with United Artists had not been a financial success—or an artistic one. The brothers decided to return to Warners. The studio system may have rankled, but Cagney recognized that his fortune had been made there. The production company stayed intact, giving Cagney more freedom than he had before.

He had departed Warners complaining of the "blood baths" he was also being asked to perform in. It is ironic that his first role upon returning was his most maniacal and homicidal, *White Heat's* crazed Cody Jarrett. He took the role grudgingly, grumbling "It's what people want me to do. Someday, though, I'd like to make just one picture kids could go see."

If kids could see *White Heat* they would learn of the limits of mother love. Because Cagney's Cody Jarrett has, simply stated, a thing about his mother. Director Raoul Walsh was attracted to the Ivan Goff-Ben Roberts script because of his continued interest in variations of the gangster theme. Walsh never did straightforward gangster narratives; *The Roaring Twenties* treated the gangsters as a historical phenomenon of the

CHAPTER VIII

BACK TO WARNERS: THE DISMAL FIFTIES

White Heat (1949)
The West Point Story (1950)
Kiss Tomorrow Goodbye (1950)
Come Fill The Cup (1951)
Starlift (1951)
What Price Glory (1952)
A Lion Is In The Streets (1953)

prohibition era and *High Sierra* saw the gangster as the last true individualist. In *White Heat*, Walsh opted for some dimestore psychology, the gangster as an overgrown mama's boy. Cody loves his mother (Margaret Wycherly) with a passion: "I don't know what I'd do without you, Ma." After Ma's death, he quotes from her with the reverence employed by Chinese workers for the sayings of Mao. Before pulling a big job, Cody wanders through the woods, communing with Ma, talking to her spirit. When "gang member" Hank Fallon (Edmond O'Brien, in actuality a federal agent) runs into Cody, the mobster tells him, with a crazy little smile: "That was a good feeling out there, talkin' to Ma. Maybe I *am* nuts." It is one of Cagney's great moments on screen and the role is among his most audacious.

Perhaps because of his boredom with gangster roles, Cagney did

WHITE HEAT (1949). With Virginia Mayo

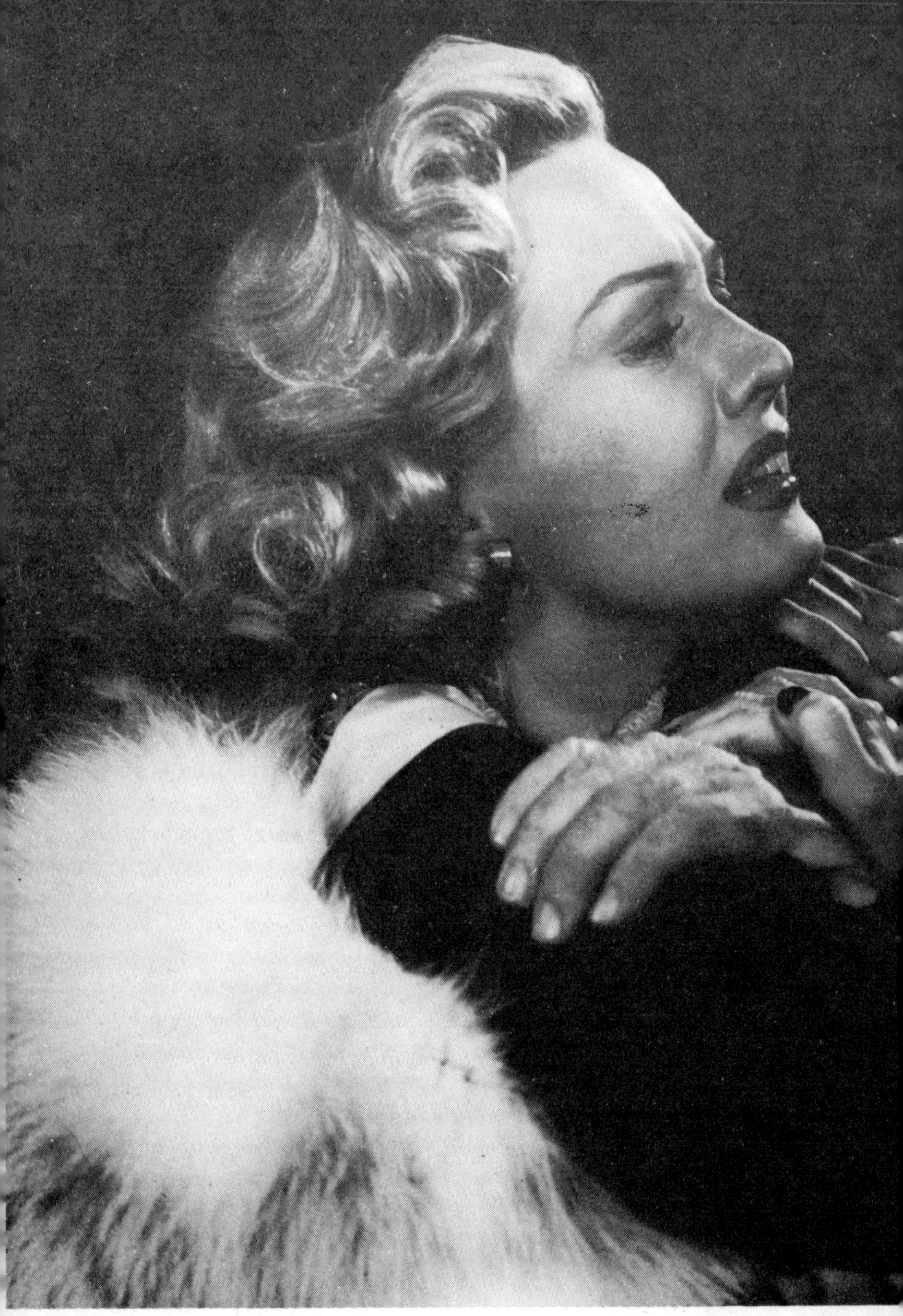

WHITE HEAT (1949). With Edmond O'Brien

his best to encourage the emphasis on Cody's tottering sanity. Let him tell it: *

I don't think you could do much more than we did in *White Heat*. The story, when I first saw it, was rather straight.

Well, we got a little into the picture [and] . . . I said to the director, Raoul Walsh, 'Raoul, let's try something. I don't know whether we'll get away with it or not: after the boy's first fit, Mama will be seated there and she will rub my head. And then I'll sit on her lap, for just a second, and put my arm around her and then walk away.'

Walsh let Cagney try it and liked what he saw; the scene stayed in.

Films and Filming, March 1959.

White Heat's other memorable moments all revolved around Cody's hang-up about Ma. Seated in the prison dining room, Cody is brought word of her death. He goes absolutely wild, throwing a blubbering fit on a histrionic level not seen since the days of silent pictures. Cody rises from his seat, starts running and weeping, howling in choked and anguished sobs. To audiences who had never seen Cagney crack, the scene was astonishing, even a little disgusting. It is a relief to see Cody placed in a straight jacket: one half-expects him to run off the screen and up the aisles of the theatre, still screaming.

Cody's end also focuses on Ma. The heist of an oil refinery's payroll has gone awry, Hank Fallon having tipped off the cops. As the law chases down Cody, having killed off everybody else in the gang, he climbs to the top of an oil tank, grinning and laughing, clearly in leave of his remaining senses. Cody is shot and decides to go out in style. He fires a volley into the oil tank. "Made it, Ma," he howls delightedly. "Top of the world!" The tank explodes, presumably blowing Cody heavenward, to be reunited with his Ma.

The film was a big hit. "The old Jimmy is back again," raved *Life*. But the old Jimmy had never been anything like this loony. A superb film, *White Heat* provided yet another example of the gradations of style Cagney could bring to a gangster role. And sadly, it was the last truly memorable picture Cagney ever made. He made other good films, such as *Man of A Thousand Faces* and *A Lion Is In The Streets* and he turned in another outstanding gangster portrayal in *Love Me Or Leave Me*. But *White Heat* was the last great picture that Cagney ever fully dominated and made his own. At fifty, Cagney was no longer offered the driving, dazzling whirlwind parts of his youth. In truth, such parts did not exist.

Actually, it was more the times than the star. The fifties were the most arid years ever for a Hollywood hounded by the Red Scare and by television. The McCarthy era drove screenwriters to jail or out of the country and removed all the social sting from the movies. The result was deadening. Political fears aside, television had introduced genuine economic peril to the film industry. Free entertainment had emptied movie houses, and picture-going, once a habit, became a "night out." Hollywood tried to attract crowds back by mounting colossal, multi-million dollar epics of a size and scope that TV could not compete with. But a steady diet of *The Robe, Solomon And Sheba*, and *Ben Hur* was impossible; these dinosaurs would eventually bankrupt the industry.

It is in this context that Cagney's rather unsatisfying career in the 1950s must be understood. Like every other major talent in Hollywood, he could only be as good as his material (and often much better). But the available material —except for such isolated gems as *The African Queen, High Noon,* and *On The Waterfront* (ideal for a younger Cagney)— was the most pedestrian in memory.

Cagney started the decade right off with a dud called *The West Point Story*, a musical that Warners hoped would take up where *Yankee Doodle Dandy* left off.

111

THE WEST POINT STORY (1950). With Cadets

THE WEST POINT STORY (1950). With Virginia Mayo

KISS TOMORROW GOODBYE (1950).
With Barton MacLane, Barbara Payton, and Ward Bond

Roy Del Ruth directed, Jule Styne and Sammy Cahn wrote the songs, and the cast included Doris Day, Gordon MacRae, Gene Nelson and Virginia Mayo. The thin story had Cagney playing a Broadway director somehow hired to direct the annual West Point Show. The film tried to warm up leftover notions from the days of *Footlight Parade* and *Here Comes The Navy;* the frantic construction of the big show and Cagney treated as a raw recruit by the cadets. Nothing worked. The songs included "Military Polka," "By The Kissing Rock" and "It Could Only Happen In Brooklyn," which Cagney performed jauntily with Virginia Mayo.

Cagney's next mistake, *Kiss Tomorrow Goodbye,* is less excusable: it originated out of his own production company. A sorry throwback, *Kiss Tomorrow Goodbye* is a stone-age gangster film with none of the psychological trimmings. Director Gordon Douglas played Harry Brown's script straight. When Cagney, as a gang leader, belts around a blonde moll (Barbara Payton), nobody is winking at the camera. Luther Adler, Ward Bond, and Barton MacLane do predictable turns as cops and heavies and even William Cagney does a bit part. He plays Cagney's brother, and not too convincingly.

With *Come Fill The Cup,* again

113

COME FILL THE CUP (1951). With Selena Royle, Raymond Massey, and Gig Young

directed by Douglas, Cagney climbed partially out of his rut. The story of an alcoholic star reporter who painfully gets back on his feet, *Come Fill The Cup* was an absorbing melodrama with some genuinely felt performances, by Cagney as newsman Lew Marsh, Phyllis Thaxter as his girlfriend, and that wonderful character actor, James Gleason, as the ex-alky who helps Marsh dry out. As long as the film concentrated on Marsh's rehabilitation, it was on safe ground. When it became muddled in a plot involving Marsh's effort to rehabilitate his

publisher's drunken nephew (Gig Young), *Come Fill The Cup* lost focus and direction. The film was never far from the kind of soap opera turned out regularly in the 1940s, but was saved by the involvement of its performers. Cagney's performance is quite moving; one suspects he was motivated by memories of what the bottle had done to his father.

After fulfilling a commitment to do a walk-on in a turkey called *Starlift*, an "all star" film in which Warners luminaries performed for the armed forces, Cagney was cast in another ill-conceived effort, this time for Twentieth Century-Fox and no less a director than John Ford.

What Price Glory, the Maxwell Anderson-Laurence Stallings play, had been made into a classic silent film by Raoul Walsh in 1926, starring Victor McLaglen and Edmund Lowe. Along with *The Big Parade* (1925) and *All Quiet On The Western Front* (1930), it was part of a great trilogy about the First World War. All three films had been released during a period in which the Great War still exercised a considerable hold upon the popular and literary imagination. So one wonders what possessed Ford to attempt a remake, six years after V-J Day and in the second year of the bewildering and unsatisfying "police action" in Korea.

Whatever his reasons, the film pleased few people. Cagney portrayed Captain Flagg, who competes with Sergeant Quirt (Dan Dailey), for the affections of Charmaine (Corinne Calvet), daughter of the innkeeper in the little French town Flagg and his troops have occupied. Cagney, who was steadily gaining weight, looked a bit long in the tooth for the part of Flagg, and Ford's conception of the picture as a semi-drama, semi-musical, a kind of half-baked *Oh, What A Lovely War!*, simply

COME FILL THE CUP (1951). On the set with pet lion, Simba

misfired. Viewed today, it is a strange and quirky film; the novel and wrong-headed work of a master director suffering from a total lapse in judgment.

Cagney's next film was another oddity, but a much more successful one. *A Lion Is In The Streets* represented another peculiar choice of material by the Cagney brothers and director Raoul Walsh. The Luther Davis script was based on a 1945 novel by Adria Locke Langley which described the rise of a Southern politician greatly resembling Huey Long. William Cagney had op-

115

WHAT PRICE GLORY (1952). With Dan Dailey

WHAT PRICE GLORY (1952). With Dan Dailey and Wally Vernon

On his farm (1955)

tioned the novel on publication, yet production didn't start until 1952, two years after the spectacular success of *All The King's Men*, which featured Broderick Crawford's bold and virtuoso performance as Willie Stark, a role clearly patterned on Long's dramatic political career. The Robert Penn Warren novel, *All The King's Men*, had achieved a reputation and fame never garnered by the Langley work, so Walsh and the brothers Cagney faced a double obstacle from the beginning.

The selection of the property might have been incomprehensible, but the final product had sur-

A LION IS IN THE STREETS (1953). With Anne Francis and Barbara Hale

prising bite. Cagney plays Hank Martin, a backwoods rabble-rouser who takes up the cause of poor farmers and discovers he has a rabid political constituency. Walsh's sure hand is evident; the action moves briskly and engrossingly. Cagney's bayou politico is a marvel of energy and guile, although his Southern accent is still more Yorkville than Baton Rouge. Barbara Hale and Anne Francis portray the women in his life, and sister Jeanne Cagney turns in a solid performance as a sharecropper's wife. (A Lion Is In The Streets was most definitely a family production: William produced and brother Edward was the story editor.) Frank McHugh also appears as a cotton gin manager, his first film with Cagney since City for Conquest in 1941.

A Lion Is In The Streets never made it out from the shadow of All The King's Men. In truth, it's not nearly the picture King's Men is, lacking the latter's broad scope. Hank Martin is not as riveting a central character as Willie Stark and simply lacks the size. Yet with all that, Walsh's film is a compelling one, and a classic case of bad timing. Rarely revived or shown on television, A Lion Is In The Streets remains the most lasting victim of Willie Stark's cunning.

118

A LION IS IN THE STREETS (1953). As Hank Martin

A 1950's portrait

Run For Cover, the Western which Cagney made next, was a less exotic choice, but it kicked off a year in which no fewer than four films featuring Cagney were released, a pace which recalled his output during the thirties. *The New York Times* wrote: "James Cagney, after two years of relative obscurity, suddenly finds himself the most sought-after actor in Hollywood." 1955 would be a banner year, but *Run For Cover* was not exactly an auspicious beginning. Director Nicholas Ray (*Rebel Without A Cause, In A Lonely Place*) took the William C. Thomas script and emphasized character over action. At fifty-six, Cagney could only benefit from this approach; his face, once bone-hard, had become puffy and Churchillian, but his energy level was still high. As the framed con turned sheriff, Cagney gave the part of Matt Dow the dimensions of age, experience, and weariness that served Ray's purposes well. But Ray's approach to the Western had definite limits, talkiness and pretension being foremost. *Run For Cover* is not the most entertaining cowboy film ever made.

More entertaining and, in fact, one of the most successful movies of 1955, was *Love Me Or Leave Me*, Charles Vidor's film biography of singer Ruth Etting. It was

CHAPTER IX

A CAGNEY REVIVAL

Run For Cover (1955)
Love Me Or Leave Me (1955)
Mister Roberts (1955)
The Seven Little Foys (1955)
Tribute To A Bad Man (1956)
These Wilder Years (1956)
Man Of A Thousand Faces (1957)
Short Cut To Hell (1957)
Never Steal Anything Small (1958)
Shake Hands With
*   The Devil (1959)*
The Gallant Hours (1960)
One, Two, Three (1961)

the first film that Cagney, who now had no studio ties at all, ever made for Metro-Goldwyn-Mayer. It was also the first time since 1931's *Smart Money* that Cagney did not receive top billing on a picture. Doris Day, playing Ruth Etting, got that credit.

But Cagney dominated the film. His portrayal of Miss Etting's gangster husband, Martin "The Gimp" Snyder (so called because of a game leg) was one of his last great creations. Snyder, a Chicago mobster who discovers Etting and promotes her career, was a most unsympathetic role for Cagney. Bitter, humorless, and pig-headed, Snyder is a nasty little man quite unprepared to handle the dimensions of his wife's success. Yet Cagney gives Snyder a vulnerabil-

RUN FOR COVER (1955). With John Derek (right)

RUN FOR COVER (1955). With Gus Schilling, Viveca Lindfors, and John Derek

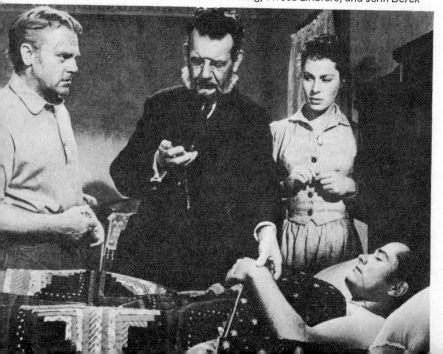

LOVE ME OR LEAVE ME (1955). With Doris Day

LOVE ME OR LEAVE ME (1955). With Robert Keith and Doris Day

MISTER ROBERTS (1955). With Jack Lemmon

ity that brings depth to the part; despite his underworld success, Snyder is clearly a loser, a cripple, physically repulsive to Etting, who stays with him out of fear and ambition.

Snyder becomes pathetic as Etting's career soars. She comes to New York to sing in the Ziegfeld Follies and Snyder tags along to "oversee" arrangements, hauling his bum leg around as though it were constructed of lead. Nobody wants him around. *Love Me Or Leave Me* tries, at least implicitly, to explain Snyder by his physical disability. The explanation is not too convincing. But Cagney is. His Snyder is twisted, mean and very, very sad. No matter how half-

MISTER ROBERTS (1955). With Henry Fonda

baked a script, Cagney could give any hoodlum flesh, blood, a brain.

Cagney's "Gimp" lost out in the 1955 Oscar race to Ernest Borgnine's Bronx butcher, *Marty*, but *Love Me Or Leave Me* copped one Academy Award, for Daniel Fuch's original story. Doris Day, surprisingly, was not nominated for "Best Actress" in what was the best performance of her career.

On the heels of his success in *Love Me Or Leave Me* came Cagney's portrayal of the Captain in the screen version of *Mister Roberts*, a highly successful Broadway comedy. The Captain was less a character role than a caricature role—a small-minded dullard of comic strip pomposity. Cagney makes it work, but the part allowed precious little leeway. The picture belongs more to Henry Fonda, repeating the title role he had introduced on Broadway, and to Jack Lemmon, making his first important screen splash as cheeky Ensign Pulver. Directed first by John Ford, who took ill during the shooting, and then by the veteran Mervyn LeRoy, *Mister Roberts* critically and financially cashed in on the built-in appeal of the hit play. *The New York Herald Tribune's* William K. Zinsser said: "As for the captain, James Cagney

THE SEVEN LITTLE FOYS (1955). With Bob Hope

makes him a remarkable specimen . . . He will be hard to forget." The public responded; *Mr. Roberts* brought Warner Brothers a profit of eight and a half million dollars.

Amazingly, *Mister Roberts* represented Cagney's first straight comedy role since 1941's dismal *The Bride Came C.O.D.* It is incredible to realize that Cagney, one of the great comic actors ever produced by this country, did no real comedy for a fourteen year span! The blame can be parcelled out in different ways, but even accepting the paucity of comic roles in the late forties and early fifties,

Cagney himself did little to encourage the impression that he was aching to play comedy. Given an independent hand, he alternated between whimsey and gangster films. But his success had not really come as a result of his gangster portrayals; the public loved him best as a shady and puckish boy on the make, relying more on wisecracks than head-breaking. Perhaps his years now made that kind of role impossible, but *Mister Roberts* and *One, Two Three*, his very last film, proved that his comic timing was unimpaired. A little addition reveals that for twenty years, Cagney made a grand total of two comedies. A lot of laughs were lost in the process.

After his revival in *Love Me Or Leave Me* and *Mister Roberts*, Cagney hit another dry spell. He closed out his 1955 labors with a "guest shot" in *The Seven Little Foys*, doing a turn as George M. Cohan. He danced with ebullience in his one scene, a hoofing bit with Bob Hope, who played Eddie Foy. The scene stole a movie which was easy prey for theft.

Nineteen fifty-six brought two failures: *Tribute To A Bad Man* and *These Wilder Years*, neither of which did anything for his reputation—or for his desire to make many more pictures. *Tribute To A Bad Man* wasted him as a mean-spirited horse rancher named Jeremy Rodock. Rodock doesn't take kindly to poachers and rustlers, usually hanging them personally. But he gradually reveals the familiar golden heart behind the crusty exterior. Whether fighting it out with his foreman or forcing horse thieves to walk barefoot ove rocky terrain, Cagney is fun to watch and Irene Papas, the great

TRIBUTE TO A BAD MAN (1956). As Jeremy Rodock

TRIBUTE TO A BAD MAN (1956).
With Irene Papas

THESE WILDER YEARS (1956).
With Barbara Stanwyck and
Betty Lou Keim

MAN OF A THOUSAND FACES (1957). With Jim Backus

Greek actress, makes her American screen debut as Rodock's girl friend, a fiery, cigar-chomping hellion. Robert Wise directed this fairly silly enterprise.

Tribute To A Bad Man is at least fun to watch; *These Wilder Years*, despite the presence of Barbara Stanwyck and Walter Pidgeon, isn't. Cagney played a millionaire, a role which suited him off-screen, but was hardly credible on-screen. Even as Cagney grew gray and paunchy, he was still most believable and compelling when crude, ambitious, and unsatisfied.

These Wilder Years was a daytime TV story: the rich man searching for his missing bastard son. He decides to adopt an unwed mother, to atone for his past sins. That plot and Roy Rowland's snail-paced direction kept people away in droves.

After these back-to-back turkeys for MGM, Cagney was thankful when a truly exciting part was offered him by Universal. The role was that of Lon Chaney, the great silent screen star who specialized in portrayals of grotesques, and the picture, *Man Of A Thousand Faces*, was a triumph. Offering

131

MAN OF A THOUSAND FACES (1957). As Lon Chaney portraying the Hunchback of

Cagney a part unlike any he had ever done before, it received widespread publicity and opened to a great critical reception. Cagney, given an extraordinary make-up job, brought forth a superb performance.

Chaney's life was a miserable one, easily susceptible to bathetic treatment. Director Joseph Pevney avoided that trap with a restrained and delicate interpretation of the actor's travails.

Born of deaf-mute parents, trapped in an unhappy and ultimately scandalous first marriage, and dead of throat cancer at forty-seven, Chaney's life was as stunted as those of his most famous creations, *The Hunchback of Notre*

Notre Dame

Dame and *The Phantom of the Opera*. Cagney captures the torture but makes Chaney a figure of great dignity, an actor projecting his off-screen turmoil into a succession of freakish, semi-human roles, roles Chaney could take refuge in. The part was a logical one for Cagney, who had become increasingly drawn to figures oper-

ating under great emotional stress. His two greatest postwar portrayals, Cody Jarrett and Martin Snyder, were physically or psychologically beaten down. Cody is insane and Snyder, a cripple, is close to the edge. Both men feel inadequate; their toughness, unlike that of Cagney's earliest gangsters, is obviously a mask.

Chaney is also driven by feelings of ineptness. The outlandish characterizations he assumed — cringing and slobbering in the bell tower—allowed Chaney to vent his frustration. Cagney's portrayal of the actor showed a keen understanding of this fact. Bosley Crowther wrote in *The New York Times:* "There is an abundance of tenderness, sensitivity and pride in his creation of the driven actor." *The New Yorker* noted that "a part like this is just about paradise for an actor of Cagney's skill." Sadly, these skills would never be used so well again.

Certainly not as a director. Cagney tried going behind the camera for the first and only time in a 1957 gangster film for Paramount called *Short Cut To Hell*. A cast of unknowns tried their best in this tired remake of *This Gun For Hire* (1941), but it was hardly worth anyone's effort. Neither was his next movie, *Never Steal Anything Small,* for Universal, a com-

133

edy with music about a stevedore who wants to be president of a longshoreman's union. Charles Lederer's direction of his own script was adequate, but four years after *On The Waterfront*, nobody was about to be sold on a musical comedy version of labor troubles. Cagney, however, turns in a very funny performance, engaging in self-parody to keep things moving and singing "Sorry, I Want a Ferrari" in a cheerful duet with Cara Williams.

It is heartening that James Cagney closed out his film career with three pictures which, if not distinguished, were at least of a quality nearly consistent with his star status. *Shake Hands With The Devil* and *The Gallant Hours* were thoughtful dramas. *One, Two, Three* allowed Cagney, most fittingly, to cap his career with a helter-skelter comedy directed by a master, Billy Wilder.

Shake Hands With The Devil centered on an American physician, one generation removed from Ireland, who visits the old country and gets deeply, if unwittingly, involved with the events of the 1921 home rule crisis. The script was by two old Cagney hands, Ivan Goff and Ben Roberts, and directed on location by Michael Anderson. It gave Cagney a chance to deal with his Irishness on screen, something he had always wanted to do—although he tried to get classic Irish drama filmed, without success. He turns in a beautiful, restrained performance as the tough-minded professor, Sean Lenihan, who talks a young American (Don Murray) into joining up with the home rule forces. Alternately bombastic, wheedling, and sly, Cagney was surrounded by British acting talent like Michael Redgrave, Cyril Cusack, and Glynis Johns. *Shake Hands With The Devil* is a modest movie, no masterpiece, yet a sleeper worthy of watching should it surface on television.

Less engrossing is *The Gallant Hours*, Robert Montgomery's study of Fleet Admiral William ("Bull") Halsey, commander of the Pacific Fleet during World War II. The film is so determined to avoid the traditional bluster of war movies that it eschews nearly all dramatics in favor of long, thoughtful stretches of dialogue as Halsey prepares for a critical battle. The results are claustrophobic and tedious; all that water and all those guns and ships—and the audience locked in Halsey's cabin. Cagney does his best, but it is not easy to stay awake through this movie.

Slumber is no problem in *One, Two, Three*, Billy Wilder's frantic

NEVER STEAL
ANYTHING SMALL (1959)
As Jake MacIllaney

NEVER STEAL ANYTHING SMALL (1959). With fellow union members

comedy about the cold war. The script, by Wilder and his long-time collaborator I. A. L. Diamond, hasn't held up all that well; the film seemed far funnier at its release in 1961 than it does now. But it did give Cagney a chance to go out with a bang, in the kind of role that he did better than anyone ever on the American screen: a brash, nonstop, wheeler-dealer with the tact of a police siren. As C. R. McNamara, a Coca Cola executive stationed in West Berlin, Cagney pulled out the stops in a performance whose pace equals his most frenetic work of the thirties. The plot, involving the disastrous marriage of his boss's hare-brained daughter (Pamela Tiffin) to an intense young Communist (Horst Buchholz), was ridiculous, but Cagney's mugging, shouting, and general hysterics carried *One, Two, Three* a lot further than it deserved. Cagney's enjoyment is obvious. Comedy had always been his specialty; it brought out the best in him, triggered all of his adrenalin. He plays McNamara with a gusto that is sadly missing in too many of his films in the fifties.

But roles like McNamara were

SHAKE HANDS WITH THE DEVIL (1959). With John Breslin and Don Murray

few and far between; Cagney decided to quit a winner. Twelve years have passed since *One, Two, Three* and Cagney has stuck to his retirement. While other actors have gone into television, as movie work continued to dry up in the sixties, Cagney has opted for agriculture, developing new kinds of fertilizer, enjoying himself thoroughly. Rumors of his illness are scotched every time he appears in public. He looks more and more like Churchill, but his waistline is the only casualty of age. A 1971 appearance at New York's Player's Club, in which he and Frank Mc-Hugh reminisced about the old days at Warners, indicated that Cagney is as sassy and full of high good humor as ever. People in that audience report that Cagney's

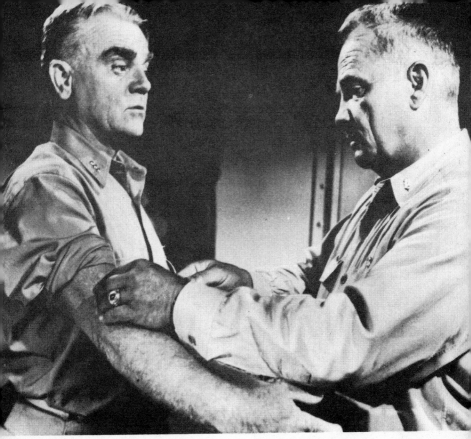

THE GALLANT HOURS (1960). With Karl Swenson

wits are unimpaired; he remains the shrewdest kid on the block.

"In this business you need enthusiasm," he told *Newsweek* in 1968. "I don't have the enthusiasm for acting anymore. Acting is not the beginning and end of everything." It never was for Cagney; he had too much self-esteem to need applause for sustenance. He reads now, especially about the Civil War, paints, and lives the life of a retired President. Except for one thing: "I get off in a room by myself, put on a recording, old, old things that had the beat . . . slip on the shoes and do four or five dances until I'm out of breath. I sit down for a while, then I try it again."

Farmer, soft-shoe dancer, Cagney is his own man. Just like we always thought he was. He hasn't betrayed his image.

ONE, TWO, THREE (1961). With Pamela Tiffin

BIBLIOGRAPHY

Agee, James. *Agee On Film*. Boston: Beacon Press, 1966.

Bergman, Andrew. *We're In The Money*. New York: New York University Press, 1971.

Bogdanovich, Peter. "Hollywood." *Esquire,* July 1972.

Cagney, James, and Martin, Peter. "How I Got This Way," *Saturday Evennig Post,* January 7, 14, 21, 1956.

Dickens, Homer. *The Films of James Cagney*. Secaucus, New Jersey; The Citadel Press, 1972.

Durant, John. "Tough, On and Off." *Collier's,* August 31, 1940.

Ferguson, Otis. "Great Guy." *The New Republic,* October 13, 1937.

"James Cagney Talking." *Films and Filming*. March 1959.

Jamison, Barbara Beach. "That's Cagney All Over." *The New York Times,* March 6, 1955.

Johnston, Alva. "They Toughened Him Up." *Woman's Home Companion,* November 1934.

"On the Current Screen." *The Literary Digest*. April 7, 1943.

Miller, Don. "James Cagney." *Films in Review,* August 1958.

Oakes, Phillip. "James Cagney." *Sight and Sound,* Winter 1958.

Pringle, Henry F. "Tough, By Request." *Collier's,* September 3, 1932.

Sennett, Ted. *Warner Brothers Presents*. New Rochelle: Arlington House, 1971.

Tuck, J. Nelson. "America's Most Lovable Bad Boy." *Read*, February 1944.

THE FILMS OF JAMES CAGNEY

The director's name appears immediately after the release date.
A (c) following the release date indicates that the film was
in color. Sp indicates Screenplay and b/o indicates based/on.

1. SINNERS' HOLIDAY. WB, 1930. *John G. Adolfi*. Sp: Harvey Thew, George Roesner, b/o play "Penny Arcade" by Marie Baumer. Cast: Grant Withers, Joan Blondell, Evalyn Knapp, Lucille LaVerne. JC is young rumrunner involved in a homicide.

2. DOORWAY TO HELL. WB, 1930. *Archie Mayo*. Sp: George Roesner, b/o story by Rowland Brown. Cast: Lew Ayres, Charles Judels, Dorothy Matthews, Leon Janney. Underworld tale, with JC as bootlegger.

3. OTHER MEN'S WOMEN. WB, 1931. *William Wellman*. Sp: William K. Wells, b/o story by Maude Fulton. Cast: Grant Withers, Mary Astor, Regis Toomey, Joan Blondell. Railroad drama, JC in bit as workman.

4. THE MILLIONAIRE. WB, 1931. *John G. Adolfi*. Sp: Julian Josephson, Maude T. Howell, b/o novel by Earl Derr Biggers. Cast: George Arliss, Evalyn Knapp, David Manners. Millionaire retires and fights boredom. JC does bit as insurance salesman.

5. THE PUBLIC ENEMY. WB, 1931. *William Wellman*. Sp: Kubee Glasmon, John Bright, b/o story by Bright. Cast: Jean Harlow, Edward Woods, Joan Blondell, Mae Clarke, Donald Cook. Rise and fall of gangster Tommy Powers. JC's big breakthrough.

6. SMART MONEY. WB, 1931. *Alfred E. Green*. Sp: Kubec Glasmon, John Bright, b/o story by Lucien Hubbard, Joseph Jackson. Cast: Edward G. Robinson, Evalyn Knapp, Boris Karloff. DA tries to trap top gambler. JC is gambler's lieutenant.

7. BLONDE CRAZY. WB, 1931. *Roy Del Ruth*. Sp: Kubec Glasmon, John Bright, b/o story by Glasmon, Bright. Cast: Joan Blondell, Louis Calhern, Noel Francis, Guy Kibbee. JC as larcenous bellhop.

8. TAXI. WB, 1932. *Roy Del Ruth*. Sp: Kubec Glasmon, John Bright, b/o play "The Blind Spot" by Kenyon Nicholson. Cast: Loretta Young, George E. Stone, Guy Kibbee. JC as leader of insurgent cab drivers, avenges brother's murder.

9. THE CROWD ROARS. WB, 1932. *Howard Hawks*. Sp: Kubec Glasmon, John Bright, Niven Busch and Seton I. Miller, b/o story by Hawks, Busch. Cast: Joan Blondell, Ann Dvorak, Eric Linden, Guy Kibbee, Frank McHugh. Two brothers on the auto racing circuit. Remade as *Indianapolis Speedway* (1939).

10. WINNER TAKE ALL. WB, 1932. *Roy Del Ruth*. Sp: Wilson Mizner, Robert Lord, b/o story by Gerald Beaumont. Cast: Marian Nixon, Virginia Bruce, Guy Kibbee, Clarence Muse. Fighter has fling with society girl, returns to first love.

11. HARD TO HANDLE. WB, 1933, *Mervyn LeRoy*. Sp: Wilson Mizner, Robert Lord, b/o story by Houston Branch. Cast: Mary Brian, Ruth Donnelly, Allen Jenkins, Claire Dodd. JC as high-pressure promoter who stages a marathon dance and can't come up with the prize money.

12. PICTURE SNATCHER. WB, 1933. *Lloyd Bacon*. Sp: Allen Rivkin, P.J. Wolfson, b/o story by Danny Ahearn. Cast: Ralph Bellamy, Patricia Ellis, Alice White. JC as ex-con hired as a roving photographer.

13. THE MAYOR OF HELL. WB, 1933. *Archie Mayo*. Sp: Edward Chodorov, b/o story by Islin Auster. Cast: Madge Evans, Allen Jenkins, Dudley Digges, Frankie Darro, Farina. JC as shyster politico shocked into action by conditions at a reformatory. Remade as *Crime School*, (1938).

14. FOOTLIGHT PARADE. WB, 1933. *Lloyd Bacon*. Sp: Manuel Seff, James Seymour. Cast: Joan Blondell, Ruby Keeler, Dick Powell, Guy Kibbee, Ruth Donnelly, Claire Dodd, Frank McHugh, Hugh Herbert. JC as musical producer in Busby Berkeley extravaganza.

15. LADY KILLER. WB, 1933. *Roy Del Ruth*. Sp: Ben Markson, Lillie Hayward, b/o story by Rosalind Keating Shaffer. Cast: Mae Clarke, Leslie Fenton, Margaret Lindsay. Comedy about gangster who flees to Hollywood and becomes a movie actor.

16. JIMMY THE GENT. WB, 1934. *Michael Curtiz*. Sp: Bertram Milhauser, b/o story by Laird Doyle, Ray Nazarro. Cast: Bette Davis, Alice White, Allen Jenkins, Arthur Hohl, Alan Dinehart. JC in frantic comedy about Jimmy Corrigan, who hunts down, or invents, heirs to fortunes.

17. HE WAS HER MAN. WB, 1934. *Lloyd Bacon*. Sp: Tom Buckingham, Niven Busch, b/o story by Robert Lord. Cast: Joan Blondell, Victor Jory, Frank Craven, Harold Huber. Safecracker frames his partners, flees country.

18. HERE COMES THE NAVY. WB, 1934. *Lloyd Bacon*. Sp: Ben Markson, Earl Baldwin, b/o story by Markson. Cast: Pat O'Brien, Gloria Stuart, Frank McHugh. Tough Chesty O'Connor joins the Navy and learns a lesson in discipline, becomes a hero.

19. THE ST. LOUIS KID. WB, 1934. *Ray Enright*. Sp: Warren Duff, Seton I. Miller, b/o story by Frederick Hazlitt Brennan. Cast: Patricia Ellis, Allen Jenkins, Robert Barrat. JC is trucker unjustly accused in murder of striking dairyman.

20. DEVIL DOGS OF THE AIR. WB, 1935. *Lloyd Bacon*. Sp: Malcolm Stuart Boylan, Earl Baldwin, b/o story by John Monk Saunders. Cast: Pat O'Brien, Margaret Lindsay, Frank McHugh, Helen Lowell. A stunt pilot from Brooklyn joins the Marine Flying Corps and alienates everybody by his arrogance.

21. G MEN. WB, 1935. *William Keighley*. Sp: Seton I. Miller, b/o story by Gregory Rogers. Cast: Robert Armstrong, Margaret Lindsay, Ann Dvorak, Barton MacLane, Lloyd Nolan. Young lawyer joins the FBI and helps destroy a major gang.

22. THE IRISH IN US. WB, 1935. *Lloyd Bacon*. Sp: Earl Baldwin, b/o story by Frank Orsatti. Cast: Pat O'Brien, Olivia De Havilland, Frank McHugh, Allen Jenkins. Three Irish brothers in New York.

23. A MIDSUMMER NIGHT'S DREAM. WB, 1935. *Max Reinhardt, William Dieterle*. Sp: Charles Kenyon, Mary McCall, Jr., b/o play by William Shakespeare. Cast: Dick Powell, Joe E. Brown, Mickey Rooney, Jean Muir, Hugh Herbert, Olivia De Havilland, Victor Jory, Frank McHugh. Lavish, all-star film version of Shakespeare classic.

24. FRISCO KID. WB, 1935. *Lloyd Bacon*. Sp: Warren Duff, Seton I. Miller, b/o story by Duff and Miller. Cast: Margaret Lindsay, Ricardo Cortez, Lily Damita, Barton MacLane. Sailor gets involved with murder on the Barbary Coast, *circa* 1890.

25. CEILING ZERO. WB, 1935. *Howard Hawks*. Sp: Frank Wead, b/o play by Wead. Cast: Pat O'Brien, June Travis, Stuart Erwin. Adventures of risk-taking pilot who indirectly causes the death of a buddy.

26. GREAT GUY. Grand National, 1936. *John G. Blystone*. Sp: Henry McCarty, Henry Johnson, James Edward Grant, Harry Ruskin, b/o stories by Grant. Cast: Mae Clarke, Edward Brophy, James Burke. Bureau of Weights and Measures official tries to head off crooks.

27. SOMETHING TO SING ABOUT. Grand National, 1937. *Victor Schertzinger*. Sp: Austin Parker, b/o story by Schertzinger. Cast: Gene Lockhart, Evelyn Daw, William Frawley, Mona Barrie. Bandleader goes to Hollywood.

28. BOY MEETS GIRL. WB, 1938. *Lloyd Bacon*. Sp: Sam and Bella Spewack, b/o play by Spewacks. Cast: Pat O'Brien, Marie Wilson, Ralph Bellamy, Dick Foran, Frank McHugh. Madcap screenwriters try to help pregnant studio waitress.

29. ANGELS WITH DIRTY FACES. WB, 1938. *Michael Curtiz*. Sp: John Wexley, Warren Duff, b/o story by Rowland Brown. Cast: Pat O'Brien, Humphrey Bogart, Ann Sheridan, George Bancroft, Leo Gorcey, Huntz Hall, Gabriel Dell, Billy Halop, Bobby Jordan. Gangster emerges from jail and returns to his old neighborhood.

30. THE OKLAHOMA KID. WB, 1939. *Lloyd Bacon*. Sp: Warren Duff, Robert Buckner, Edward E. Paramore, b/o story by Paramore and Wally Klein. Cast: Humphrey Bogart, Rosemary Lane, Donald Crisp. Son revenges father's death on the Cherokee Strip.

31. EACH DAWN I DIE. WB, 1939. *William Keighley*. Sp. Norman Reilly Raine, Warren Duff, b/o novel by Jerome Odlum. Cast: George Raft, Jane Bryan, George Bancroft, Victor Jory, Maxie Rosenbloom. Newspaper reporter is framed and sent to prison.

32. THE ROARING TWENTIES. WB, 1939. *Raoul Walsh*. Sp: Jerry Wald, Richard Macaulay, Robert Rossen, b/o story by Mark Hellinger, Cast: Humphrey Bogart, Priscilla Lane, Jeffrey Lynn, Gladys George, Frank McHugh. Rise and fall of bootlegger, from Prohibition through the Great Crash.

33. THE FIGHTING 69TH. WB, 1940. *William Keighley*. Sp: Norman Reilly Raine, Fred Niblo, Jr., Dean Franklin. Cast: Pat O'Brien, George Brent, Jeffrey Lynn, Dick Foran, Frank McHugh. Saga of famous World War I fighting unit, JC as tough recruit.

34. TORRID ZONE. WB, 1940. *William Keighley*. Sp: Richard Macaulay, Jerry Wald. Cast: Pat O'Brien, Ann Sheridan, Helen Vinson, Andy Devine. Romance-adventure set on a South American plantation.

35. CITY FOR CONQUEST. WB, 1941. *Anatole Litvak*. Sp: John Wexley, b/o novel by Aben Kandel. Cast: Ann Sheridan, Arthur Kennedy, Frank Craven, Donald Crisp, Frank McHugh, Anthony Quinn. Promising fighter goes blind after ring accident.

36. THE STRAWBERRY BLONDE. WB, 1941. *Raoul Walsh*. Sp: Julius and Philip Epstein, b/o play by James Hagan. Cast: Olivia de Havilland, Rita Hayworth, Jack Carson, Alan Hale, George Tobias. Tale of a dentist's romances, set in the late nineteenth century. Remade as musical *One Sunday Afternoon* in 1948.

37. THE BRIDE CAME C.O.D. WB, 1941. *William Keighley*. Sp: Julius and Philip Epstein, b/o story by Kenneth Earl, M.M. Musselman. Cast: Bette Davis, Stuart Erwin, Jack Carson, George Tobias. Romance between cocky pilot and runaway heiress.

38. CAPTAINS OF THE CLOUDS. WB, 1942. *Michael Curtiz*, (C) Sp: Arthur T. Horman, Richard Macaulay, Norman Reilly Raine, b/o story by Horman and Roland Gillett. Cast: Dennis Morgan, Brenda Marshall, Alan Hale, George Tobias. American joins Canadian RAF.

39. YANKEE DOODLE DANDY. WB, 1942. *Michael Curtiz*. Sp: Robert Buckner, Edmund Joseph, b/o story by Buckner. Cast: Joan Leslie, Walter Huston, Richard Whorf, George Tobias, Irene Manning, Rosemary DeCamp, Jeanne Cagney, S.Z. Sakall. Musical biography of George M. Cohan.

40. JOHNNY COME LATELY. UA, 1943. *William K. Howard*. Sp: John Van Druten, b/o novel by Louis Bromfield. Cast: Grace George, Marjorie Main, Hattie McDaniel, Edward McNamara. Hobo helps lady newspaper publisher fight corrupt interests.

41. BLOOD ON THE SUN. UA, 1945. *Frank Lloyd*. Sp: Lester Cole, b/o story by Garrett Fort. Cast: Sylvia Sidney, Wallace Ford, Rosemary De Camp, Robert Armstrong. American newspaperman searches for secret Japanese war plans during 1920s.

42. 13 RUE MADELEINE. Fox, 1946. *Henry Hathaway*. Sp: John Monks, Jr., Sy Bartlett. Cast: Richard Conte, Annabella, Frank Latimore, Walter Abel. American espionage agents operating in France, one of whom is actually working for the Nazis.

43. THE TIME OF YOUR LIFE. UA, 1948. *H.C. Potter,* Sp: Nathaniel Curtis, b/o play by William Saroyan. Cast: William Bendix, Wayne Morris, Jeanne Cagney, Broderick Crawford, Paul Draper. Philosophizing and dreaming by regulars at a San Francisco bar.

44. WHITE HEAT. WB, 1949. *Raoul Walsh.* Sp: Ivan Goff, Ben Roberts, b/o story by Virginia Kellogg. Cast: Virginia Mayo, Edmond O'Brien, Margaret Wycherly, Steve Cochran. Mother-obsessed hoodlum causes mayhem.

45. THE WEST POINT STORY. WB, 1950. *Roy Del Ruth.* Sp: John Monks, Jr., Charles Hoffman, Irving Wallace, b/o story by Wallace. Cast: Virginia Mayo, Doris Day, Gene Nelson, Gordon MacRae, Alan Hale, Jr., Roland Winters. Broadway director stages West Point musical show.

46. KISS TOMORROW GOODBYE. WB, 1950. *Gordon Douglas.* Sp: Harry Brown, b/o novel by Horace McCoy. Cast: Barbara Payton, Luther Adler, Ward Bond, Helena Carter, Steve Brodie. JC as another gang leader.

47. COME FILL THE CUP. WB, 1951. *Gordon Douglas.* Sp: Ivan Goff, Ben Roberts, b/o novel by Harlan Ware. Cast: Phyllis Thaxter, Raymond Massey, James Gleason, Gig Young. Alcoholic reporter fights his way back from the gutter.

48. STARLIFT. WB, 1951. *Roy Del Ruth.* Sp: John Klorer, Karl Kamb, b/o story by Klorer. Cast: Gordon MacRae, Virginia Mayo, Doris Day, Gene Nelson, Ruth Roman, plus top Warners stars. All-star vehicle for Warners' contract players, entertaining servicemen.

49. WHAT PRICE GLORY. Fox, 1952. *John Ford.* (C) Sp: Phoebe and Henry Ephron, b/o play by Maxwell Anderson and Laurence Stallings. Cast: Corinne Calvet, Dan Dailey, William Demarest, Craig Hill, Robert Wagner. Two World War I doughboys compete for the hand of an innkeeper's daughter.

50. A LION IS IN THE STREETS. WB, 1953. *Raoul Walsh.* (C) Sp. Luther Davis, b/o novel by Adria Locke Langley. Cast: Barbara Hale, Anne Francis, Warner Anderson, Jeanne Cagney, Frank McHugh. Rise of backwoods Southern politician.

51. RUN FOR COVER. Par., 1955. *Nicholas Ray.* (C) Sp: Winston Miller. b/o story by Harriet Frank, Jr. and Irving Ravetch. Cast: Viveca Lindfors, John Derek, Jean Hersholt, Grant Withers. JC as ex-con sheriff in talky Western.

52. LOVE ME OR LEAVE ME. MGM, 1955. *Charles Vidor.* (C) Sp: Daniel Fuchs, Isobel Lennart, b/o story by Fuchs. Cast: Doris Day, Cameron Mitchell, Robert Keith, Tom Tully, Harry Bellaver. Biography of singer Ruth Etting, with JC as her mobster husband.

53. MISTER ROBERTS. WB, 1955. *John Ford, Mervyn Le Roy.* (C) Sp: Frank Nugent, Joshua Logan, b/o play by Logan & Thomas Heggen. Cast: Henry Fonda, Jack Lemmon, William Powell, Ward Bond, Betsy Palmer. Comedy set on Navy cargo ship stationed in the South Pacific. JC as despotic captain.

54. THE SEVEN LITTLE FOYS. Par., 1955. *Melville Shavelson.* (C) Sp: Melville Shavelson, Jack Rose. Cast: Bob Hope, Milly Vitale, George Tobias. Biography of hoofer Eddie Foy, with JC doing bit as George M. Cohan.

55. TRIBUTE TO A BAD MAN. MGM, 1956. *Robert Wise.* (C) Sp: Michael Blankfort, b/o story by Jack Schaefer. Cast: Don Dubbins, Stephen McNally, Irene Papas, Vic Morrow. Story of hardbitten horse rancher.

56. THESE WILDER YEARS. MGM, 1956. *Roy Rowland.* Sp: Frank Fenton, b/o story by Ralph Wheelwright. Cast: Barbara Stanwyck, Walter Pidgeon, Betty Lou Kein, Edward Andrews. Rich man sets out to find his illegitimate son.

57. MAN OF A THOUSAND FACES. Univ- Int'l, 1957. *Joseph Pevney.* Sp: R. Wright Campbell, Ivan Goff, Ben Roberts, b/o story by Ralph Wheelwright. Cast: Dorothy Malone, Jane Greer, Marjorie Rambeau, Jim Backus. Biography of film actor Lon Chaney.

58. SHORT CUT TO HELL. Par. 1957. *James Cagney.* Sp: Ted Berkman, Raphael Blau, from screenplay by W.R. Burnett, b/o novel by Graham Greene. Cast: Georgann Johnson, William Bishop, Peter Baldwin, Robert Ivers. JC's only directorial effort, a low budget remake of *This Gun For Hire,* about a professional killer. JC appeared on film only to introduce the cast of unknowns, who have remained unknown.

59. NEVER STEAL ANYTHING SMALL. Univ.-Int'l, 1958. *Charles Lederer.* (C) Sp: Charles Lederer, b/o play by Maxwell Anderson and Rouben Mamoulian. Cast: Shirley Jones, Roger Smith, Cara Williams, Nehemiah Persoff. Tough, crooked longshoreman goes after union presidency.

60. SHAKE HANDS WITH THE DEVIL. 1959. *Michael Anderson.* Sp:

Ivan Goff, Ben Roberts, b/o novel by Reardon Conner. Cast: Don Murray, Dana Wynter, Glynis Johns, Michael Redgrave, Sybil Thorndike, Cyril Cusack. JC as surgeon who gets involved in Irish home rule struggle during the early 1920s.

61. THE GALLANT HOURS. 1960. *Robert Montgomery.* Sp: Beirne Lay, Frank D. Gilroy. Cast: Dennis Weaver, Ward Costello, Richard Jaeckel. Saga of Admiral Halsey's battles in the Pacific during the early days of World War II.

62. ONE, TWO, THREE. 1961. *Billy Wilder.* (C) Sp: Wilder, I.A.L. Diamond, b/o play by Ferenc Molnar. Cast: Horst Buchholz, Pamela Tiffin, Arlene Francis, Lilo Pulver. Comedy about American Coca-Cola executive stationed in West Berlin.

INDEX

(Page numbers italicized indicate photographs)

151

152